mustsees
Las Vegas

© JUPITERIMAGES/ Creatas / Alamy

MICHELIN

mustsees **Las Vegas**

Editorial Manager	Jonathan P. Gilbert
Principal Writer	Lark Ellen Gould
Production Manager	Natasha G. George
Cartography	Peter Wrenn
Photo Editor	Yoshimi Kanazawa
Proofreader	Hannah Witchell
Layout	Jonathan P. Gilbert, Natasha G. George
Interior Design	Chris Bell, cbdesign
Cover Design	Chris Bell, cbdesign, Natasha G. George

Contact Us	Michelin Travel and Lifestyle
	One Parkway South
	Greenville, SC 29615
	USA
	www.michelintravel.com
	michelin.guides@us.michelin.com
	Michelin TravelPartner
	Hannay House
	39 Clarendon Road
	Watford, Herts WD17 1JA
	UK
	(01923) 205 240
	www.ViaMichelin.com
	travelpubsales@uk.michelin.com

Special Sales	For information regarding bulk sales, customized editions and premium sales, please contact our Customer Service Departments:	
	USA	1-800-432-6277
	UK	(01923) 205 240
	Canada	1-800-361-8236

Michelin Apa Publications Ltd

A joint venture between Michelin and Langenscheidt

58 Borough High Street, London SE1 1XF, United Kingdom

No part of this publication may be reproduced in any form without the prior permission of the publisher.

© 2011 Michelin Apa Publications Ltd
ISBN 978-1-907099-41-0
Printed: August 2011
Printed and bound: Himmer, Germany

Note to the reader:
While every effort is made to ensure that all information printed in this guide is correct and up-to-date, Michelin Apa Publications Ltd. accepts no liability for any direct, indirect or consequential losses howsoever caused so far as such can be excluded by law. Admission prices listed for sights in this guide are for a single adult, unless otherwise specified.

The strip viewed from Mandalay Bay

Introduction

Las Vegas:
The Neon Jungle

Must See

917.93635
MIC

p 84

Must Do

Must Eat

Must Stay

Must Know

TABLE OF CONTENTS

5

★★★ATTRACTIONS

Unmissable attractions awarded three stars in this guide include:

Bellagio p 22

MGM Resorts International

Death Valley National Park p 96

©PhotoDisc

CityCenter Las Vegas p 33

Darrin Bush/Las Vegas News Bureau

Grand Canyon National Park p 93

©Ryan Morgan/iStockphoto.com

MUST KNOW

The Venetian p 23

The Strip p 26

Wynn Las Vegas p 24

Hoover Dam p 92

STAR ATTRACTIONS

★★★ ATTRACTIONS

Unmissable sights in and around Vegas

For more than 75 years people have used the Michelin stars to take the guesswork out of travel. Our star-rating system helps you make the best decision on where to go, what to do, and what to see.

★★★	**Absolutely Must See**
★★	**Really Must See**
★	**Must See**
No Star	**See**

 **ACTIVITIES**

For every Vegas casino and stunning Grand Canyon vista there are a thousand more activities. We recommend every activity in this guide, but our top picks are highlighted with the Michelin Man logo.
Look-out for the Michelin Man throughout the guide for the top activities.

STAR ATTRACTIONS

CALENDAR OF EVENTS

Listed below is a selection of Las Vegas' most popular annual events. Please note that dates may change from year to year. For more detailed information, contact the *Las Vegas Convention and Visitors Authority: 702-892-0711; www.lvcva.com*.

January

Martin Luther King Jr. Parade
Downtown Las Vegas
702-440-6400
www.kingweeklasvegas.com

February

Chinese New Year Celebration
Chinatown Plaza,
4255 Spring Mountain Rd.
702-221-8448
www.lvchinatown.com

March

St. Patrick's Celebration
Fremont St.
702-678-5777
www.vegasexperience.com
NASCAR Races
Las Vegas Motor Speedway
800-644-4444
www.lvms.com

April

Mardi Gras Festival
Fremont St.
702-678-5777
www.vegasexperience.com
Las Vegas Craft Show
Cashman Center
www.stevepowers.com
Clark County Fair and Rodeo
Fairgrounds in Logondale
888-876-FAIR
www.ccfair.com
Rhythm & Blues Festival
Government Amphitheater
800-969-VEGAS
www.yourjazz.com

May

Helldorado Days Rodeo Western Fest
Downtown Rodeo Arena
702-229-6776
www.elkshelldorado.com

December: National Finals Rodeo

© Darren Carroll/Sports Illustrated/Getty Images

December: *New Year's Eve in Vegas*

Darrin Bush/Las Vegas News Bureau

Cinco de Mayo Festival
Lindo Michoacan
702-735-6828
www.lindomichoacan.com
Vegas Uncork'd
Venues around the city
877-884-8993
www.vegasuncorked.com

September
San Gennaro Street Fair
Flamingo Rd. Valley View Blvd.
702-286-4944
www.sangennarofeast.net
Mexican Independence Day
Lorenzi Park, W. Washington St.
702-649-1198
Greek Food Festival
St. John's Greek Orthodox Church
702-248-3896
Ho'olaule'a Pacific Island Festival
Henderson Events Plaza
702-267-2171
www.travelnevada.com

October
Oktoberfest
Hofbräuhaus
702-853-BEER
Art in the Park
Bicentennial Park, Boulder City
702-294-1611
www.artinthepark.org

Renaissance Festival
Desert Breeze Park at Spring
Mountain Rd. and Durango.
702-455-8200
www.lvrenfair.com

November
Professional Bullriders
World Finals
Thomas & Mack Center
University of Nevada, Las Vegas
www.pbrnow.com
Steve Powers Great
Las Vegas Craft Show
Cashman Center
www.stevepowers.com

December
National Finals Rodeo
Thomas & Mack Center University
of Nevada, Las Vegas
888-637-7633
www.nfr-rodeo.com
International Gem
& Jewelry Show
Cashman Center
301-294-1640
www.intergem.net
New Year's Eve in Vegas
Fremont St. 702-678-5777
www.las-vegas-new-years-eve.com
Las Vegas Convention & Visitors
Authority. 702-892-0711

PRACTICAL INFORMATION

WHEN TO GO

If you love sun, that's just one of the many excesses you'll find in Las Vegas. With an average of 307 sunny days a year, the city usually sees only four inches of rain annually (September is the rainiest month, though some locals swear it is July) with the months of September and October and then March to May simply sublime. Granted, you won't find the humidity (average 29 percent) here that your hair or skin might seek, but your sinuses will thank you. Las Vegas sits in the middle of the Mojave Desert and summers can see temperatures climbing as high as 120°F during a summer's day, dropping only 20 degrees at night. Spring and autumn bring daytime temperatures averaging in the 70s and 80s. In the winter, temperatures may drop below freezing, although the average high is between 50–60°F. When it comes to numbers, if you hate crowds, don't come during national holidays, especially when there's a three-day weekend involved. Certain conventions and events also bring in huge numbers of people, raising rates sky-high. From late February to early May, and then again from mid-September to mid-November, Las Vegas is simply divine. Bring a good pair of walking shoes or even hiking boots because you will want to be outside, whether that means walking The Strip (see p26) or hiking the desert. Pool poppers will want to check ahead with the hotel to make sure there is a four-season soaking spot on the premises and scenesters will want to check out the "day life" to be found at the adult pool parties all over town. The least crowded time to hit The Strip is traditionally the week or two before Christmas through a day or two before New Year's Eve. The buffet lines are at their shortest and the hotels roll out some of their best promotions during that time. However, because of recent declines in visitor numbers resulting from rising gas prices, recession spending trends and reduced air traffic, visitors will be amazed to find out just how affordable a stay at a top Strip property can be no matter what the season.

KNOW BEFORE YOU GO
Useful Websites

www.visitlasvegas.com - Official tourism website of Las Vegas.
www.lasvegasadvisor.com - Vegas expert Anthony Curtis gives the inside eye on Vegas' top spots.
www.vegas.com - An easy to navigate and up-to-date travel site.
www.lasvegas.com - From hotels to gambling, it all starts here.

Average Seasonal Temperatures in Las Vegas			
	Jan	**Apr**	**July**	**Oct**
Avg. High	57°F/14°C	78°F/26°C	104°F/40°C	81°F/27°C
Avg. Low	34°F/1°C	44°F/7°C	68°F/20°C	46°F/8°C

Visitor Information

Before you go, check with the following organizations to obtain the *Las Vegas Official Visitor Guide*, as well as maps and information on accommodations, dining, shopping, festivals and recreation:

Las Vegas Visitor Information Center – Operated by the Las Vegas Convention & Visitors Authority 3150 Paradise Road, Las Vegas, NV 89109. *702-892-0711; www.lvcva.com. Open year-round daily 8am–5pm.*

Las Vegas Chamber of Commerce – 6671 Las Vegas Blvd. South, # 300, Las Vegas, NV 89119. *702- 641-5822; www.lvchamber.com.*

International Visitors

In addition to the tourism offices throughout Nevada, visitors from outside the US can obtain information from the website of the **Las Vegas Convention and Visitors Authority** *(www.lvcva.com)* or from the US embassy or consulate in their country of residence. For a complete list of American consulates and embassies abroad, visit the website for the **Department of State, Bureau of Consular Affairs** *(http://USembassy.gov).*

Entry Requirements – Travelers entering the United States under the **Visa Waiver Program (VWP)** must present a machine-readable passport to enter the US without a visa; otherwise, a US visa is required. Required entry documents must include biometric identifiers *(fingerscans—full Visa Waiver Program requirements can be found at http://travel. state.gov).* Citizens of countries participating in the VWP are permitted to enter the US for

general business or tourism for up to 90 days without a visa. For a list of countries participating in the VWP, contact the US consulate in your country of residence. Citizens of non-participating countries must have a visa, a valid passport and round-trip ticket. As of December 31, 2006, travelers to and from Canada must present a passport or other secure, accepted document to enter or re-enter the US. Inoculations are generally not required, but check with the US embassy or consulate. All citizens of non-VWP-participating countries must have a visitor's visa.

US Customs – All articles brought into the US must be declared at the time of entry. Prohibited items include produce and plant material, firearms and ammunition (if not for sporting purposes), meat/poultry products. For information contact the US embassy or consulate before departing, or the **US Customs Service** *(877-287-8667; www.customs.treas.gov).*

Accessibility

Disabled Travelers – Federal law requires that businesses (including hotels and restaurants) provide access for the disabled, devices for the hearing impaired and designated parking spaces. For information, contact the **Society for Accessible Travel and Hospitality (SATH):** 347 Fifth Ave., Suite 610, New York NY 10016 *(212-447-7284; www.sath.org).* All **national parks** have facilities for the disabled and offer free or discounted passes *(National Park Service, Office of Public Inquiries, P.O. Box 37127, Room 1013, Washington, DC 20013-7127; 202-208-4747; www.nps.gov).*

PRACTICAL INFORMATION

For train or bus travel contact **Amtrak** *(800-872-7245 or 800-523-6590/TDD; www.amtrak.com)* or Greyhound *(800-752-4841or 800-345-3109/TDD; www.grey hound.com)*. Make reservations for hand-controlled rental cars in advance with the rental company.

Senior Citizens – Many hotels, attractions and restaurants offer discounts to visitors aged 62 or older (proof of age may be required. Also check out *www.aarp.com.)*

GETTING THERE
By Air

McCarran International Airport (LAS), located 4 miles southeast of The Strip, handles domestic and international flights *(5757 Wayne Newton Blvd.; 702-261-5743; www.mccarran.com)*. Information desks or kiosks are located throughout the airport. **Shuttles and taxis** can be found outside door 11 in the baggage claim area. **Bell Trans shuttles** leave from door 9 every 10 minutes *($6.50 to Strip hotels, $8-$12 to off-Strip hotels; reservations: 739-7990 or 800-274-7433)*. Taxis to Strip hotels average $18–$20 *(cash only)*.

There's a consolidated **car-rental depot** located off-site; you can catch one of the many continuous buses to the lot where 11 car companies have rental desks. The **Ground Transportation Center** near baggage claim has information about shuttles, car rentals and limousine transport.

By Bus

There's no Amtrak train service here, but a **Greyhound** bus station is located downtown *(200 S. Main St.; 702-384-9561 or 800-231-2222; www.greyhound.com)*.

By Car

Direct interstate access to Las Vegas is via I-15 from Butte, Montana and Southern California.

Driving in the US – Visitors bearing valid driver's licenses issued by their country of residence need not obtain an **International Driver's License**. However, drivers must carry vehicle registration and/or rental contract, and proof of automobile insurance at all times. Gasoline is sold by the gallon (more than $4 at press time). Vehicles in the US are driven on the right-hand side of the road.

Southwest airplane leaving from McCarran Airport in front of Luxor Las Vegas

Glenn Pinkerton/Las Vegas News Bureau

MUST KNOW

Car Rental		
Car Rental Company	*⌖* **Reservations**	**Internet**
Alamo	800-327-9633	www.alamo.com
Avis	800-331-1212	www.avis.com
Budget	800-527-0700	www.drivebudget.com
Dollar	800-800-4000	www.dollar.com
Enterprise	800-325-8007	www.enterprise.com
Hertz	800-654-3131	www.hertz.com
National	800-227-7368	www.nationalcar.com
Thrifty	800-331-4200	www.thrifty.com

GETTING AROUND
Walking The Strip

The Las Vegas Strip *(Las Vegas Blvd.)* is just over 4 miles long, running south, from Russell Road (by Mandalay Bay) north to Charleston Boulevard, and downtown. The Strip is crossed by five major streets: Russell, Tropicana, Flamingo, Spring Mountain and Sahara.

Overhead walkways connect several properties: New York-New York, the MGM Grand, the Tropicana and Excalibur; Caesars Palace, Bellagio and Bally's; The Venetian, TI; and Encore/Wynn Las Vegas to Fashion Show Mall.

By Bus

Double-decker **Deuce** buses run from the **Downtown Transportation Center** *(Stewart Ave. & Casino Center Blvd.)* down **The Strip** past **Mandalay Bay** and the Four Seasons about every 8 to 17 minutes depending on time of day, 24/7, stopping at designated bus stops deemed popular for visitors. Buses to The Strip are $2 one way; pay when you get on *(exact change required)*. Buses off The Strip are $1

each way *(exact change required)*. Timetables for the **Citizen Area Transit buses (CAT)**, which go all over the city, are available on buses and in the hotels. *(For routes and schedules: 702-228-7433 or www.rtcsouthernnevada.com.)*

By Taxi

Taxis line up outside all hotel entrances. Cabs cannot be hailed on the street; summon them at cab stands or by calling the cab company.

By Monorail

The **Las Vegas Monorail** *(www.lvmonorail.com)* stops at 11 hotel-resort properties on The Strip and less directly connects passengers with another 16. It begins its 4-mile, 14-minute north-south run at the **Sahara Hotel** *(Sahara Ave.)* and ends up at the **MGM Grand** *(Tropicana Ave.)*. *Fares are $5 one-way, and $12 for a one-day pass ($28 for three days)*. Discounted promotions and packages are available and noted on the website and through tour companies. The route, with stops at the **Las Vegas Hilton**, the

Las Vegas Monorail

Las Vegas News Bureau

Convention Center, Wynn, Harrah's/ Imperial Palace, Flamingo/Caesars Palace and Bally's/Paris, and MGM Grand, runs parallel to The Strip behind the hotels and offers great views of the backlots. Note that the walk from the monorail platform to the casino or The Strip is usually a long one.

By Car

Don't drive unless you know the back entrances to the hotels and can avoid The Strip, which tends to be gridlocked at all hours. All The Strip hotels have **valet parking** *(standard tip for valet attendants is $1–2).*

The Ranch Experience

If you have a hankering for some Old West cattle roping, camping out, or riding off into the sunset (often with a campfire dinner), here are some places to contact:

+ **Sagebrush Ranch**
  702-256-6049
+ **Bonnie Springs Ranch**
  702-875-4191
+ **Mt. Charleston Riding Stables** *702-387-2457*

BASIC INFORMATION
Accommodations

For a list of suggested accommodations, see Hotels. For the best deal, book your room in advance. Room rates are dependent on occupancy; the higher the occupancy at a property, the more the rooms will cost. For that reason, prices fluctuate from day to day.

In light of the recession, it's possible to get a luxury hotel room or suite at a budget price by doing your research, although on holidays you might end up paying top prices for a low-rent room. As a rule of thumb, prices are lower during the week and in low-occupancy months (traditionally during the summer, before Christmas and in January). Rates are highest at hotels on The Strip, but the convenience of being near the action is worth the extra cost. Rooms downtown, and especially off The Strip, will be quieter, less expensive and often a better value.

Las Vegas Convention & Visitors Authority Reservation Service: *800-332-5333.*
Campgrounds are available at **Mt. Charleston, Dolomite Campgrounds** and **Kyle Canyon Campgrounds**; all are run by the *U.S. Forest Service's Spring Mountains National Recreation division (702-515-5400; www.fs. fed.us).* There is also camping in **Red Rock Canyon** *(702 515-5350; www.redrockcanyonlv.org).*
RV Parks in Las Vegas have full hook-ups and accept pets. Rates generally run $40+ per night. Reservations are recommended.
California RV Park – *Stewart Ave.*

Property	🖉 Phone/Website	Property	🖉 Phone/Website
Best Western	800-528-1234 www.bestwestern.com	Hyatt	800-233-1234 www.hyatt.com
Comfort, Clarion & Quality Inns	800-228-5150 www.comfortinn.com	ITT Sheraton	800-325-3535 www.sheraton.com
Crowne Plaza	800-227-6963 www.crowneplaza.com	Marriott	800-228-9290 www.marriott.com
Days Inn	800-325-2525 www.daysinn.com	Ramada	800-228-2828 www.ramada.com
Hilton	800-445-8667 www.hilton.com	Dolce Hotels	888-WW-DOLCE www.dolce.com
Holiday Inn	800-465-4329 www.holiday-inn.com	Westin	800-937-8461 www.westin.com

at Main St. 702-385-1222 or 800-634-6505.
Circus Circus KOA Park –
500 Circus Circus Dr. 702-733-9707, or 800-562-7270.

Business Hours

Many services run 24-hours. These include grocery stores, drug stores, gas stations, coffee shops, wedding chapels and much more (you can even find laudramats and hair salons open in the midnight hours). Casinos and many of their restaurants, bars and nightclubs run all hours, as do their bank cages. Government offices and bank offices have standard daytime hours: an exception is the wedding license bureau downtown, which is open 8am–midnight every day of the week.

Communications

Telephones – Most hotels will charge a fee for all phone calls made from the guestroom, so it is best to use a mobile. High-speed WiFi is available in most hotel rooms for a charge of around

Important Phone Numbers	
(24hrs)	
Police (non-emergency)	🖉 **311**
24-hour Pharmacies:	
Walgreens, 1101 Las Vegas Blvd. S	🖉 702-471-6844
Sav-On, 3250 Las Vegas Blvd.	🖉 702-643-8538
Poison Control Center, Clark County	🖉 800-446-6179
Time (commercial information service)	🖉 702-853-1212

$13 per day, and is often free in convention and conferences areas. To reach another Las Vegas hotel from the casino you are in, simply pick up a house phone located near the bank of public phones and dial zero. Hotel operators are usually willing to oblige. **Area codes** – To make a long-distance call, dial: 1+area code+ seven-digit number. **Las Vegas Area: 702.**

Discounts

Discounts are delivered to coupon rippers, newsletter subscribers and slot players. Coupon pages exist in nearly all the top free publications such as **What's On, Las Vegas 24/7, Where** and all manner of print that can be grabbed from visitor centers, taxi cabs and concierge desks. Find $2 to 20 percent discounts for anything from a breakfast buffet to a 'copter ride to the 'Canyon. A top spot to check is **LasVegasAdvisor.com** where promos and deals abound with a newsletter subscription. The site specializes in keeping an inside edge on the best deals in town. Joining a casino "players club" and playing for points at your favorite resort beats all when it comes to to racking up freebies.

Discount passes – Las Vegas is rife with packaging companies bundling tours, admissions and discount coupons into handy, value-laden exploration tools. **Explorer Pass** *866-794-5227;*

www.explorerpass.com/lasvegas **VisitTicket** *www.visiticket.com* **Las Vegas Power Pass** *866-988-8687, www.city-discovery.com*

Electricity

Voltage in the US is 120 volts AC, 60 Hz. Foreign-made appliances may need AC adapters (available at specialty travel and electronics stores) as well as North American flat-blade plugs.

Media

Newspapers and Magazines – Consult the city's major daily newspaper, the *Las Vegas Review Journal (www.lvrj.com)*, for dining and entertainment news.

Money

Currency Exchange – Exchange currency at downtown banks and **McCarran Airport**. For cash transfers use **Western Union** *(800-325-6000; www.westernunion.com).*

Cash and Cheques – US banks, stores, restaurants and hotels accept traveler's checks with picture identification.

Lost and Stolen – **American Express**, 800-528-4800 **Diners Club**, 800-234-6377 **MasterCard**, 800-307-7309 **VISA**, 800-336-8472

Smoking

A law passed in 2006 set up a smoking ban in Las Vegas anywhere near the serving of food. That means all restaurants and most indoor public spaces are now smoke free. Casinos remain untouched by the laws.

Sports

Yes, there is life after gaming and much of it is outdoors. From golf,

Measurement Equivalents									
Degrees Fahrenheit	95°	86°	77°	68°	59°	50°	41°	32°	23°	14°
Degrees Celsius	35°	30°	25°	20°	15°	10°	5°	0°	-5°	-10°

1 inch = 2.5 centimeters	1 foot = 30.5 centimeters
1 mile = 1.6 kilometers	1 pound = 0.4 kilograms
1 quart = 0.9 liters	1 gallon = 3.8 liters

tennis and cycling to boating at Lake Mead, rock climbing at **Red Rock Canyon**, or skiing on **Mt. Charleston**, there's no lack of things to do.

Boxing – Las Vegas has become a boxing mecca with championship fights held at the **MGM Grand, Mandalay Bay, Caesars Palace** and **Wynn Las Vegas**. Ringside seats can cost as much as $1,500 while the "cheap" seats go for $100–$200.

Car Racing – A 1,500-acre motorsports complex, **Las Vegas Motor Speedway** *(7000 Las Vegas Blvd. N.; 702-644-4444; www.lvms.com)*, can accommodate up to 107,000 spectators. Highlights include the annual UAW-DaimlerChrysler 400 *(Mar)*, and the National Hot Rod Association drag-racing events *(Apr & Oct)*.

College Sports – Fans can watch the University of Las Vegas **Runnin' Rebels** play football and basketball *(campus bordered by Maryland Pkwy., Tropicana Ave., Paradise Rd & Flamingo Rd.)*. Basketball games are held at the Thomas & Mack Center *(4505 Maryland Pkwy.)*. Catch football matches at **Sam Boyd Stadium** *(7000 Russell Rd.)*. Tickets: *702-739-3267 or www.unlvtickets.com*.

Golf – Las Vegas currently boasts more than 50 golf courses, designed by such big-name players as **Arnold Palmer, Robert Trent**

> ### It's Showtime!
> At Vegas casinos, showtimes, performances and prices change often. Check with the **theater box office** and with half-price kiosks at malls and along The Strip for the latest.

Jones Sr., and **Pete Dye**. For websites with up-to-the-minute information, reviews and tee time booking capabilities, try *www.lasvegasgolf.com* and *www.lasvegasgolfcourses.com*.

Rodeo – Every year, the **National Finals Rodeo (NFR)** comes to town in December and the Professional Bull Riders World Finals happen in November. *(702-895-3900; www.nfr-rodeo.com)*.

Taxes
Prices displayed do not include sales tax (7.75% in Vegas), which is not reimbursable.

Time
Las Vegas operates on Pacific Standard Time.

Tipping
It is customary to give waiters 15–20% of the sum, porters $1 per bag, chamber maids $1 per day, and cab drivers 15% of the fare.

PRACTICAL INFORMATION

LAS VEGAS

Sin City, Kitsch Town USA, Lost Wages, Neon Wasteland, call it what you will. But whatever name you attach to Las Vegas, it's hyperlinked to a call to action. Las Vegas is the **City that Never Sleeps,** that never stops churning the frenetic energy heard in the clanking sounds of slot machines, the exchange calls of table dealers, the echoes of singing fountains and wails of bellowing nymphs. But for all its names, nuances and in-your-face answers to appetites of every ilk it is a place like no place else. Take a whirl down the glass and sculptured canyon that is the Las Vegas Strip. Wander its backyard pool parks of daring day life, its cavernous spas of royal pampering treatments, its endless line-up of star chef restaurants and shameless show rooms of luxury products ready to rouse the senses of the sheikhs and celebrities. But look beyond the G-strings and glitter and find a path of your own. Behind the neon is a desert of unwavering beauty.

Just beyond the city, by the forbidding sands of the Mojave Desert, Las Vegas has gone from being a quiet spot in the desert to a world-class resort destination. The city's colorful history starts 12,000 years ago in a marsh covered with lush vegetation. As eons passed, the marsh receded, the rivers disappeared. What remained was an arid, parched landscape of the hardiest of plants and animals. Water trapped underground in the geological strata of the valley sporadically surfaced to nourish the plants and create an oasis in the desert. Protected from discovery by the harsh surrounds the site that would become Las Vegas was hidden for centuries from all but isolated tribes of Native Americans.

On Christmas Day in 1829, a Mexican trader, **Antonio Armijo**, leading a 60-man party along the Spanish Trail to Los Angeles, veered about 100 miles northeast of present-day Vegas. Searching for water for the group, **Raphael Rivera**, an experienced 18-year-old Mexican scout, discovered the sweet artisian wells of Las Vegas Springs. The name stuck: Las Vegas is Spanish for *the meadows*.

CityCenter Tram

Darrin Bush/Las Vegas News Bureau

The Strip and Bellagio fountains viewed from Cosmopolitan of Las Vegas

The **Mormons** were the first group to settle in the area: In 1855 members of the Church of Latter-Day Saints built a fort out of sun-dried adobe bricks near Las Vegas Creek *(see Historic Sites)*; but it was the advent of the railroad that led to the founding of Las Vegas on May 15, 1905. That was the day that the **Union Pacific** auctioned off 1,200 lots in an area that is now the Fremont Street Experience—a traffic-free, pedestrian mall. Nevada became the first state to legalize casino-style **gambling**; and then, reluctantly, the last western state to outlaw it during Prohibition in the first decade of the 20C. At midnight on October 1, 1910, a strict anti-gambling law took effect in Nevada. Gambling was legalized again in 1931. For many years thereafter, the Mafia ruled Las Vegas. During the early years of The Strip, no holds were barred to attract gamblers—there was no cover charge, no state speed limit, no sales tax, no waiting period for marriages, no state income tax, and no regulation of gambling, as there is today, however nominal.

In 1966, when billionaire Howard Hughes arrived in the city to live at the Desert Inn (which he purchased), the Nevada legislature finally passed a law allowing publicly traded corporations to obtain gambling licenses. Gradually, legally obtained capital started to flow into the city. Consequently, in the 21C, the financial foundations of Las Vegas are firmly anchored in legitimate corporations, which spare no expense trying to outdo one another to lure gamblers and conventioneers by building one fabulous megaresort after another.

Cashing In On Casinos

By far the most celebrated of the early Las Vegas resorts was the **Flamingo Hotel**, a classy "carpet joint" modeled on the fancy resort hotels in Miami and built by **Benjamin "Bugsy" Siegel**, a member of the Meyer Lansky crime organization. With its giant pink neon sign and motif replicas of pink flamingos, the Flamingo opened on New Year's Eve, 1946. Six months later, Siegel was murdered by an unknown gunman, most likely attached to the Mob.

THE NEON JUNGLE

CASINOS

Vegas just wouldn't be Vegas without its casinos. The gaming houses that once lit Las Vegas Boulevard with flashing neon have now mushroomed into spectacular themed megaresorts incorporating hotels, restaurants, art museums, animal habitats, and pretty much anything else you can imagine—and some things you can't! Here you'll find reproductions of the Eiffel Tower in Paris, Venice's Grand Canal, and the Sphinx in Egypt. Ogle all you want. If there was ever an eye-popping experience, Vegas is it! *For a legend of price listings $$$$$ for hotels, see Hotels.*

Bellagio★★★

3600 Las Vegas Blvd. S.
702-693-7111 or 888-987-7111.
ww.bellagiolasvegas.com.
3,930 rooms. $$$$$

Fine art, gardens, fashion; these are hardly things that you used to associate with a casino in Las Vegas. But that was before this hotel's vision changed the landscape of the gambling mecca. When Steve Wynn opened the $1.7-billion Bellagio in October 1998 (it's now owned by MGM Mirage), he created a place of ideal beauty and comfort. Considered one of the most opulent upscale resorts in the world, this 36-story property was inspired by the village of Bellagio on the shores of Lake Como in northern Italy.

An eight-acre lake, the scene of spectacular **fountain and light shows★★**, graces the front of the complex. Inside, the hotel's casino is arguably the most chic in town; try your hand at a game of Texas Hold 'em or 7-Card Stud in the smoke-free Poker Room or dine with a view at Prime, or Picasso, or even Olives and have the fountains and lake all to yourself.

The cavernous 116,000 square foot casino rarely suffers from smoky air. The atmosphere stays clear and scented, perhaps assisted by the spring-like beauty of the lobby with a firmament of glass flowers, each handblown by artist Dale Chihuly. The stunning botanical art abloom in the adjacent conservatory changes its colors and settings with each season.

Bellagio at dusk

Bob Brye/Las Vegas News Bureau

The Venetian★★★

3355 Las Vegas Blvd. S.
702-414-4405 or 888-283-6423.
www.venetian.com.
7,025 suites. $$$$$

Never been to Venice? Don't despair! **St. Mark's Square**, the stately **Doge's Palace**, the **Campanile** and the **Grand Canal**★★ are all closer than you think—at the elegant Venetian in Las Vegas. The world's largest all-suite hotel and convention complex, the Venetian boosted its suite count to a staggering 4,049 units in June 2003 when it opened its Venezia Tower. Designed to painstakingly reproduce the city of Venice, the hotel is located on the site where the venerable Sands Hotel Casino—a Las Vegas institution and the home of the famed Rat Pack—stood from 1952 until it was imploded in 1996. The casino is decked out with reproductions of famous frescoes on the ceilings and marble on the floors. More than 122 table games include a semi-private area for high-stakes Baccarat.

At the Venetian you can update your wardrobe at the **Grand Canal Shoppes** *(see Shopping)*, which house 75 exclusive retailers, or take a gondola ride—complete with serenade—through the canal that winds around the shops and

The Venetian

Las Vegas News Bureau

restaurants and in waters along the frontage of The Strip. Be sure to save up for a dinner at Bouchon or Valentino's *(see Restaurants)*.

The Venetian takes showmanship quite seriously and has added two permanent blockbusters to its nightly roster of stage productions. **Blue Man Group** puts a new spin on its colorful and candid performance each evening and **Phantom of the Opera** was given new life with its own ambient opera house of special effects and a cast that keeps the show sweet and moving within a 90-minute frame, no intermissions.

The $1.2-billion property opened in May 1999 with designs on becoming the largest hotel complex in the world and in 2008

CASINOS

it succeeded. The newest addition to The Strip is the **Palazzo Hotel** at the Venetian. It boasts a 50-story luxury tower with approximately 3,025 lavish and large suites, which gives the Venetian the distinction of being the largest hotel in the US (7,025 suites). Find signature dining with such restaurants as CUT by Wolfgang Puck, a sprawling mall of Fifth Avenue-style retail anchored by Barney's New York, and the West Coast home to the "Jersey Boys" straight from Broadway.

If Venetian is the hyperactive young adult, eager to play in a world full of possibility, Palazzo is the impressive and powerful uncle who was to the manner born. Palazzo keeps a refined profile evident immediately in the spacious casino that feels more like an elegant oversized living room than a crowded gaming parlor.

With more than 16 restaurants going hungry is not an option. Although, similar to the adjacent Venetian, Palazzo does not have a buffet. Rather it has names like Lagasse, Trotter and Batali joining Puck in the limelight of culinary splash. In addition there is casual dining at the Grand Lux and Japanese-Brazilian fare at Sushisamba.

As the largest hotel campus in the world, the Venetian and Palazzo also share what is probably the largest hotel spa in the world at **Canyon Ranch SpaClub**. Where most hotel spas run around 20,000 square feet and brag if the area sprawls to 30,000, Canyon Ranch SpaClub in Las Vegas counts an improbable 134,000 square feet (think more than two football fields) of sublime pampering. The spa connects the Venetian

and the Palazzo around a series of pools and gardens and adds such features as the "Aquavana," a European-inspired suite of thermal cabins, experiential showers, cold rooms and thermal bathing experiences to add to the resort's overall theme of opulence.

A stay in the Chairman Suite at Palazzo brings with it four bedrooms, its own pool and garden of Italian statuary, a private putting green and outdoor rainfall shower. Through French doors from the terrace find a baby grand piano by the wet bar and marble fireplace. Your bill for the night? $15,000.

Wynn Las Vegas★★★

3131 Las Vegas Blvd. S.
702-770-7000 or 888-320-7123.
www.wynnlasvegas.com.
2,716 rooms. $$$$$

No volcanoes, white tigers, wayward pirates or syncopated fountains mark Steve Wynn's latest Las Vegas opus; this curvilinear mocha-colored glass tower is all about class. The "man who made Las Vegas" opened his signature 50-story Strip resort on April 28, 2005 on the site of the old Desert Inn. As you enter the hotel from The Strip, you'll find yourself in a blooming, light-filled solarium promenade, teeming with design boutiques. Walk down the promenade to see the **Lake of Dreams★★**, where a 140-foot mountain of cascading water dazzles spectators with a multimedia special-effects show twice an hour. Press into the small hall to watch, or enjoy the spectacle while sipping Dom Perignon at the ring-side seats at the two **Parasol lounges**, named

Wynn and Encore

Las Vegas News Bureau

for the whimsical parasol light fixtures suspended from their ceilings. A destination in its own right, the $2.7-billion resort boasts 18 restaurants; a Tom Fazio-designed golf course ($500 per round at peak times); and a 2,087-seat theater that stages a water-themed Cirque-style production called Le Reve.

Encore opened in 2008 as a broader and more luxurious twin to Wynn, connected by a glamour-packed corridor of dining, boutiques and clubs. The daylife and nightlife in the Encore pool areas has become a legendary part of the party culture in this town. Shoppers and browsers will be duly impressed by the on-site Ferrari-Maserati showroom and souvenir store (you may have to stand in line for a look but you can always jump into the souvenir shop and

buy a set of Porsche pencils for $6). You'll also find plenty of designer shopping at the **Wynn Esplanade** *(see Shopping)*, where labels like Oscar de la Renta, Manolo Blahnik, Chanel, and Dior abound. December 2008 brings the opening of Wynn's next oeuvre, Encore: an elegant 2,034-suite hotel attached to Wynn and featuring five new restaurants, a smattering of retail, a new ultra nightclub, and a spa all as part of a greater Wynn complex.

Caesars Palace★★

3570 Las Vegas Blvd. S.
702-731-7110 or 800-634-6661.
www.caesars.com.
3,327 rooms. $$$$

Even Julius would have been proud of this majestic hotel that can rightfully claim to be the first theme resort in Vegas. Caesars

Chariot of the Goods

♦ Caesars is the gateway to the $100-million **Forum Shops**, a chi-chi mall covered by a domed ceiling that changes from day to night *(see Shopping)*. You'll think you're walking down the streets of Rome when you wander amid columns, piazzas and statuary.

♦ Journey into the land Cleopatra would have died for: at **Qua Spa**, you can have a treatment that douses your body in an aromatic massage and then dresses your skin in a design of Swarovski crystals.

CASINOS

The Strip★★★

The city's greatest concentration of resorts and casinos lies along a 4-mile stretch of **Las Vegas Boulevard** known as The Strip. Beginning at the Stratosphere and reaching south to Mandalay Bay *(2000–4000 blocks of Las Vegas Blvd.)*, The Strip is a carnival of sensational architecture and streetside displays. In 2009 the largest project ever to hit The Strip opened: The MGM Mirage CityCenter. This $10-billion city within a city is also the world's leading "green project". Measuring 76 acres at mid-Strip, with 6,300 rooms spread across four hotels, 500,000 square feet of retail, dining and entertainment and casino space to match, this marvel also features forward design by leading architects.

Palace, which opened in 1966, cost $25 million to build (they've added more than $1 billion in renovations since) and stretches over 85 acres. This Greco-Roman extravaganza encompasses spectacular fountains, three casinos, 12 restaurants, a health spa, a beauty salon, the **Appian Way** shopping area, tennis courts and 4 entertainment lounges. Within its 129,000 square feet of luxe casino space, Caesars offers slot machines that accept denominations of 5¢ to $500.

In 1998 Caesars added a 4.5-acre outdoor **Garden of the Gods** with three swimming pools. In 2003 the property experienced a renaissance when the new 4,300-seat **Colosseum** showroom opened, now boasting **Bette Midler**, Cher, Jerry Seinfeld and Elton John as regular headliners.

In 2005, the 900-room Augustus Tower and Spa opened and brought with it star restaurants for celebrity chefs Guy Savoy, Bradley Ogden and Bobby Flay.

In 2009, Caesars plans to open its newest addition: the 23-story, 665-room **Octavius Tower** as part of a $1 billion expansion that includes three super luxury villas and a trio of lavish pools complementing the gardens.

Caesars Palace

Caesars Entertainment

Sphinx and Pyramid of Luxor Las Vegas

Las Vegas News Bureau

Luxor Las Vegas★★

3900 Las Vegas Blvd. S.
702-262-4000 or 800-288-1000.
www.luxor.com. 4,692 rooms. $$$

Imagine ancient Egypt in this 30-story **pyramid**, with a 29-million-cubic-foot atrium at its apex. Fabulous reproductions of artifacts from Luxor, Egypt as well as the Karnak Temple line the walls of the hotel, along with copies of hieroglyphics found in Egypt's Valley of the Kings.

You'll enter the hotel beneath a massive 10-story replica of the **Sphinx**. From there, you'll be transported to your room by "inclinator," an elevator that travels up the interior slope of the 350-foot pyramid at 39 degrees.

But, even the kingdoms of Pharaohs must change and this one is morphing into a vision of what Tut would have wished for in the afterlife.

Luxor has managed to blend hip LA with cool Karnak and the result is a choreographed explosion of new restaurants, shows, nightclubs and attractions bringing this aging pyramid into the 21C.

Lights in the Kingdom

♦ By night, a 315,000-watt laser beam—the **Xenon Light★★**—shoots out from the top of the pyramid; it's visible as far as 250 miles away in Los Angeles.

♦ In the evening hours magician **Criss Angel** comes to life with haunting mindgames of mysticism and illusion.

♦ Over in the casino is the world's largest atrium, carved into a cityscape and ancient medina.

Find **LAX**, a star-powered nightclub backed by DJ AM and Christina Aguilera, which took over from RA. Aurora is a new lobby lounge full of special effects lighting based on the Aurora Borealis. Noir Bar is a nightclub, tagged as an ultra-exclusive nightspot catering only to the most elite clientele; while Cathouse offers boudoir dining. For some odd, non-clubby amusement check out the permanent exhibits at Luxor: Bodies and Titanic. Both venues bring history and hidden facts to life with expensive and impressive displays built to remember.

CASINOS

27

MGM Grand

Las Vegas News Bureau

That's Entertainment

The **MGM Grand** has two main showrooms. The first theater was the longtime home of the city's first special-effects spectacle, EFX, which closed in December 2002 and reopened in 2004 as the new home of KÀ, Cirque du Soleil's most dramatic production to date. The second, 700-seat Hollywood Theatre presents star headliners like Craig Ferguson, Lewis Black and David Copperfield, 365 days a year.

MGM Grand★★

3799 Las Vegas Blvd. S.
702-891-1111 or 800-646-7787.
www.mgmgrand.com.
5,034 rooms. $$$

Considered one of the largest hotels in the world, this 114-acre city within a city really roars with amenities: gourmet and specialty restaurants; a 6.6-acre pool and spa complex; Studio 54 nightclub; the 17,157-seat MGM Grand Garden for superstar concerts and world championship sporting events, Studio Walk shopping, an engaging **CSI: The Experience★** crime scene investigation attraction, and **CBS Television City★**, featuring a studio walk with screening rooms for TV show pilots.

In 2006 MGM created two new hotels within its grand complex: **Skylofts** and Signature. Skylofts is an exclusive hotel within a hotel. Taking up the penthouse floors of the emerald tower, 51 one and two-bedroom suites have the views, the dedicated concierge service, the amenity- and gadget-packed abodes and the privacy. This comes at a hefty price of course, but this is Vegas at its finest. Aquaphiles will find the six-acre Grand Pool complex alluring. It has five pools, plenty of waterfalls and features, as well as a lazy river running around the rim—all open all year. For scene seekers, daylife can be found at Wet Republic where the barely-in-a-bikini crowd comes to sun and soak.

Lions and Lions and Lions… Oh My!

In MGM Grand's casino, gaming takes on a whole new meaning. Besides 3,500 slot machines and 165 table games, the hotel has real MGM lions right in the middle of the casino. Kids from 8 to 80 will enjoy the **Lion Habitat★**, located near Studio 54 in the middle of the gaming area. Lions romp through the three-story naturalistic structure and walk right over your head (thanks to the wonders of bullet-proof safety glass) in full view. When there are cubs, you can even have a picture taken with them!

Where The Animals Play

The Mirage is home to **The Secret Garden of Siegfried & Roya**, a lush sanctuary for six rare breeds of exotic cats, including the duo's rare white tigers *(see Animal Acts)*. The habitat provides a way for Siegfried & Roy (conservationists who have established breeding programs on three continents to save the white tiger and white lion from extinction) to share the results of their efforts with the public. Adjoining the Secret Garden is the **Dolphin Habitat**, a breeding and research facility for Atlantic bottlenose dolphins. Guests can meet and frolic with the dolphins up close in a new Trainer for a Day program offered by the hotel.

The Mirage★★

3400 Las Vegas Blvd. S.
702-791-7111 or 800-627-6667.
www.themirage.com.
3,050 rooms. $$$

You'll think you're seeing things when you check in at the Mirage—in front of a 20,000-gallon aquarium full of colorful fish (and a few sharks). A few steps into the hotel, you'll find a Polynesian fantasy of lush gardens under a 90-foot-high glass-enclosed atrium filled with royal palms and foliage. The rain-forest theme extends into the casino, where the blackjack tables have the best rules in town. Outside, there's a lagoon with waterfalls and a **volcano★★** that

erupts every 30 minutes after dark with effects and an orchestral score. If this sounds like a tropical paradise, that's what it's supposed to be. This resort, which opened in November 1989 to the tune of $630 million, is credited with being the property that triggered the boom of themed megaresorts up and down the Las Vegas Strip in the early to mid-1990s. Here you can see exotic wildlife in lush habitats, thanks to entertainers Siegfried & Roy, or with **Terry Fator**, enjoy an evening with some very talented singing puppets.

LOVE, a Beatles-themed Cirque du Soleil production has been packing the house since opening in June 2006.

The Mirage

Las Vegas News Bureau

CASINOS

New York-New York for Sports Fans & Bar Flies

ESPN Zone – A premier sports and dining complex made up of three individual, yet integrated, components. The first is the Studio Grill, where you can enjoy generous portions of American fare. Then there's the Screening Room, featuring two 14-inch screens surrounded by a dozen 36-inch monitors for broadcasting live sports events. Last, but not least, the Sports Arena boasts 10,000 square feet of interactive and competitive games. **Coyote Ugly** – This southern-style bar and dance saloon is patterned after the original Coyote Ugly bar in New York City, the one that inspired the blockbuster movie produced by Jerry Bruckheimer. Each night, sexy bartenders climb atop the bar to perform a bold show filled with stunts ranging from fire-blowing to body shots and choreographed dance numbers—and the best part is, you can join in the fun!

New York-New York★★

3790 Las Vegas Blvd. S.
702-740-6969 or 800-693-6763.
www.nynyhotelcasino.com.
2,024 rooms. $$$

Start spreading the news: this stellar resort—the tallest casino in Nevada at 47 stories (529 feet)—depicts the familiar New York skyline with re-creations of familiar landmarks. A replica of the **Statue of Liberty★★** is the resort's signature; surrounded by 12 New York City towers, including a version of the **Empire State Building** (47 stories), the Century Building (41 stories) and the Chrysler Building (40 stories). There's even a 300-foot-long model of the **Brooklyn Bridge★**. The **Manhattan Express**, a Coney Island-style roller coaster, travels around the skyscrapers at speeds of up to 60mph. Around the crowded 84,000-square-foot casino, you'll walk by familiar New York sites such as Park Avenue, Central Park, and Times Square. New York-NewYork is a great place to experience tasty apple martinis; a Coney Island arcade; a bar with dueling pianists; an authentic Irish pub; and Cirque du Soleil's sexiest show ever, *Zumanity*.
See Productions.

New York-New York

Las Vegas News Bureau

Paris Las Vegas★★

3655 Las Vegas Blvd. S.
702-946-7000 or 888-266-5687.
www.parislv.com.
2,916 rooms. $$$

Eiffel Tower Paris Las Vegas

Bob Brye/Las Vegas News Bureau

Ooh-la-la! If you want to experience the City of Lights and can't afford the air fare, give this hotel a go. Although its namesake city lies across the ocean, Paris Las Vegas strives to capture the essence of Paris, France. Here you can dine 100 feet above The Strip in a 50-story replica of the **Eiffel Tower★★**, or whiz up in a glass elevator to an observation deck overlooking the Las Vegas Valley (not to be confused with the Left Bank). The place even looks like Paris, with a reproduction of the **Arc de Triomphe**, and façades of **L'Opéra**, the **Louvre** and the **Hôtel de Ville**. The resort opened in September 1999 with Catherine Deneuve, Charles Aznavour and Michel LeGrand in attendance. It cost a cool $790 million to build and its authenticity extends from the French phrases spoken by the employees, to the security guards clad in gendarme uniforms. Three legs of the Eiffel Tower rest on the floor of the casino, whose Parisian streetscapes provide the oh-so-chic setting for 90 table games and more than 1,700 slot machines. Paris is connected to its sister property, Bally's, by Le Boulevard, a Parisian-style shopping district, complete with cobblestone streets, street lamps and authentic French boutiques and eateries. If you're a pastry lover, don't miss Lenôtre for chocolate and J.J.'s Boulangerie for fresh bread. The property also boasts one of the city's best and most atmospheric buffets, a showroom, and a wonderful Mandara spa. For the show, it's "The Producers" with a changing cast of characters playing Bialistock and Bloom. Now part of Harrah's Corp., which also owns Caesars, Rio, Bally's, Flamingo and Imperial Palace among others, guests can charge to their room from all Harrah's hotels.

Champagne, Sparkling Wine, Cigars?

A must-not-miss on Le Boulevard at Paris Las Vegas is **Napoleon's Champagne Bar**, which offers a selection of more than 100 champagnes and sparkling wines by the bottle and by the glass, complemented by a light menu of hors d'oeuvres. For smokers, Napoleon's features a cigar bar with a walk-in humidor. Live entertainment nightly makes this a popular night spot.

CASINOS

THEhotel at Mandalay Bay★★

3950 Las Vegas Blvd. S.
702-632-7000 or 877-632-7000.
www.mandalaybay.com.
1,120 rooms. $$$$

Although it's attached to Mandalay Bay, this all-suites hotel, opened in December 2003, has its own separate entrance and individual spirit. Beyond the Art Deco lobby you'll find the exceptional Bathhouse spa on the second floor, and Alain Ducasse's acclaimed restaurant, Mix, on the 64th floor—accessible by its own glass elevator. There's also a sky lounge with a terrace for lingering over the lights of the city. The average suite measures 750 square feet and comes with three plasma televisions, high-speed internet, a deep soaking tub, and a wonderfully comfy bed. Mandalay Bay links to Luxor through the **Mandalay Place** shopping complex *(see Shopping),* located along a 310-foot-long sky bridge.

Treasure Island Las Vegas★★

3300 Las Vegas Blvd. S.
at Spring Mountain Rd.
702-894-7111 or 800-288-7206.
www.treasureislandlasvegas.com.
2,900 rooms. $$$

When Steve Wynn first opened this hotel in 1993, the drawbridge from The Strip led to the world of Robert Louis Stevenson's 1883 adventure novel *Treasure Island.* Outside, waves lapped at a replica of a small island village. Inside, overflowing treasure chests lined the walls, carpets were patterned

Treasure Island

Las Vegas News Bureau

with jewels and gold doubloons, and stolen treasure hung above the casino tables.

The booty is now gone from the rafters—and so is the name. Treasure Island was rebranded as TI in 2004 and the famed Pirate's Battle in front of the hotel was traded for a steamy song-and-dance show performed by sexy girls—billed as the **Sirens of TI** —in wet, skin-tight rags. The ancient Mediterranean fishing village frontage is still there, although it's now used as nightclub and dining terraces.

The Bathhouse

3950 Las Vegas Blvd. S. 702-632-7000 or 877-632-7000. www.the hotelatmandalaybay.com.
The $25-million, 14,000-square-foot **Bathhouse** spa has been receiving attention for its austere design, incorporating ultrasuede-lined walls, charcoal-colored slate, cool glass, and lots of falling water within its textured geometric spaces. The two-story complex contains hot and cold plunge pools, eucalyptus steam rooms, redwood saunas, and dimly lit relaxation rooms.

CityCenter Las Vegas★★

3780 Las Vegas Blvd. S.
702-590-7757.
www.citycenter.com.

You cannot mention American mega-projects and innovations in architecture, environmental design and hospitality trendsetting without stopping to take in the grand intentions—and results —of CityCenter Las Vegas. The behemoth footprint on the Las Vegas Strip encompasses four hotels and residential towers so far, a huge casino, brag-worthy spas, endless dining venues and an upscale mall that could as easily be found in Abu Dhabi or Dubai.

This was to be the signature of what Las Vegas money—in the right hands—can do when dirt started to move in 2006. The ambitious 76-acre site between Monte Carlo and Bellagio hired a battalion of famous architects (think Rafael Viñoly, Helmut Jahn, Pelli Clarke Pelli, Daniel Libeskind, David Rockwell, London's Foster + Partners, Kohn Pedersen Fox Associates, and Gensler) and asked them to start drawing into a whole, a mini city within a city that would

shine so bright it would stun those who pass it. The result, after opening in 2010 and spending $11 billion is nothing short of spectacular.

Aria is the centerpiece, a sweeping half-moon curve that anchors the "city" with a 61-story, 4,004-room casino property (the casino, at 160,000 square feet, is the only one at CityCenter). The rooms are all futuristic oeuvres in glass with touch modules that operate all moving components at bedside. There's a bi-level, 80,000-square-foot spa with such gratis amenities as a toxin-defying salt chamber and Korean-style heated granite cubbies for healing.

In dining CityCenter has all the flash a top resort in Vegas requires. That means showplaces for Chicago's Shawn McClain, Michael Mina, Jean-Georges Vongerichten, Julian Serrano, Sirio Maccioni, Pierre Gagnaire and others.

But what about next door? Connected to Aria is Vdara, a condohotel concept in which every room is ready to be lived in with floor to ceiling glass views and plenty of panache all within a non-smoking 57-floor, 1,150-room

CityCenter Las Vegas

Brian Jones/AP Photo/Las Vegas News Bureau

tower that is the leading model for eco-hospitality in Las Vegas. Even the two-story Vdara spa boasts an eco-environment of organic products and mindful, meditative surroundings.

Up the path is Mandarin Oriental Las Vegas bringing all the design and built-in comforts of the Hong Kong-based brand. The tower presents mostly private residences but operates 392 hotel rooms that keep the whimsical Adam Tihany signature found at MO's around the world. The spa is an attraction here with relaxation stations looking through floor to ceiling windows over the neon. For dining, it's a Michelin-starred chef, of course. Twist is chef Pierre Gagnaire's first foray into the US.

Other CityCenter spots are residences and developments yet to open, ever a work in progress. Art, however, is a theme not to be forsaken in the making. Commissioned works by the world's top artists (Maya Lin, Jenny Holzer, Nancy Rubins, and Frank Stella, among others) present a continuous line of eye candy. In fact, the art to be found is so compelling that one can actually follow a walking tour through a specially designed smartphone app for a worthy break from sights along The Strip.

☘ Cosmopolitan of Las Vegas★

3708 Las Vegas Blvd. S.
702-698-7000 or 877-551-7778.
www.cosmopolitanlasvegas.com.
2,995 rooms. $$$$

Cosmopolitan … its name betrays urban sophistication, or perhaps a sensual cocktail ordered in just the right manner. And the double glass towers on the north edge of the imposing CityCenter skyline do not disappoint.

Cosmopolitan is Las Vegas' newest mega hotel/casino with 2,995 residential-style rooms and a hefty price tag of $3.9 billion. It had a checkered start with plans to become a luxury condo tower before succumbing to bankruptcies, bank take-overs and the usual recession mayhem. When it opened finally in December 2010, it was dressed to impress with columns of blinking video art gracing the lobby, all wrapped in a sumptuous web of crystal gauze.

According to CEO John Unwin, it's all supposed to be about art, urban edginess and wow factors at every vantage—and the hotel keeps its promise with rotating presentations of up and coming artists of refreshing and whimsical approach and some permanent collections of, say, a room-size, ruby red stiletto healed shoe along an unassuming corridor and vending machine dispensing contemporary artistic oeuvres from 1950s-era cigarette machines for $5 a pull. For all its glitz and trendiness, the hotel aims at the middle market with large, design-forward, amenity-packed rooms offering open terraces over The Strip for rates similar to those found at Luxor and Treasure Island.

Three rooftop pools, a club with day and night scenes and live concerts, and some dozen name restaurants keep the energy flowing throughout this eight-acre footprint in prime location on the Las Vegas Strip.

REST OF THE BEST: MORE CASINOS

Las Vegas never sleeps and that has been true, too, for the cranes and backhoes along the Strip that have built ever more fantastical structures along the Strip – most recently CityCenter, the largest green-built hotel project on the planet. And they all do two things very well: get you to spend money and make your head swirl.

Circus Circus★

2880 Las Vegas Blvd. S.
702-734-0410 or 800-634-3450.
www.circuscircus.com.
4,000 rooms. $

Opened in 1968, Circus Circus was the city's first gaming establishment to offer entertainment for all ages. Initially there was a casino and a carnival midway, but no hotel rooms. The first 400 rooms were built in 1972. Today the casino occupies the main floor, while the second floor hosts carnival games, arcade games and a 🎪 **circus arena**. The 🎪 **Adventuredome** indoor theme park was added in 1993 (*see For Kids*). Today, the show must go on and the daily roster of circus acts that made this property famous continue with an impressive array of talent that comes from all over the world to make it in Las Vegas. It is possible to pull slots and hit your soft 12 while trapeze artists fly above you. For those who want in on the game, Circus Circus is one of the few casinos in town that offer free gaming lessons at set times each day. Hungry guests should check out the buffet—still one of the best deals in town.

Excalibur★

3850 Las Vegas Blvd. S.
702-597-7777 or 800-937-7777.
www.excalibur-casino.com.
4,008 rooms. $$

Ever dream of traveling back in time to an age of jousting knights? Enter the world of King Arthur (a great place to bring the kids) via this sparkling medieval castle. In **King Arthur's Arena** you can eat with your hands and cheer the action during the Tournament of Kings. Keeping with the Camelot theme, the hotel's shopping mall

Circus Circus

Las Vegas News Bureau

Excalibur

is a medieval village. There's also a male dance revue that would likely make King Arthur blush. Excalibur remains friendly to families, despite some growing up it has done recently. Following a bottom to top redo of the rooms, the property recently completed a redesign of the pool area, with four pools, brand spanking new cabanas, fire pits, sun decks and a secluded relaxation pool. There are ten cabanas designed especially for those traveling with children. Hungry swimmers can have food delivered via the new poolside restaurant, Drenched. Cabana rentals start at $125.

Mandalay Bay Resort & Casino★

3950 Las Vegas Blvd. S.
702-632-7777 or 877-632-7000.
www.mandalaybay.com.
3,660 rooms. $$

Life is a beach at Mandalay Bay. This tropical-themed resort possesses the only sand-and-surf beach on The Strip. Besides its casino, the property boasts an 11-acre 🏊 **lagoon**, a three-quarter-mile lazy river ride, 15 restaurants,

nightclubs, shops, **Shark Reef★★** aquarium *(see Animal Acts)*, and the renowned House of Blues (don't miss their Sunday Gospel brunch). You can take a monorail from Mandalay Bay to its sister properties, Luxor and Excalibur. Rooms here are large and luxurious and offer fabulous views of The Strip. Summer turns the resort into ground zero for scene-style fun with one of The Strip's few European bathing pools and summer rock concerts that can be experienced from the beach pool.

Planet Hollywood★

3667 Las Vegas Blvd. S.
702-791-7827 or 877-333-WISH.
www.planethollywood.com.
2,600 rooms. $$$

The 1001 Nights of Aladdin has morphed into the Swarovski crystal lights of Planet Hollywood, officially opened in September 2007 with a glamor-laden lobby, clean edged casino floor and suites that play upon the lives of celebrities, each with its own mini-museum of memorabilia. LA is everywhere here, from Pink's Hot Dogs in the Race and Sports Book Lounge to KOI Restaurant, straight from

La Cienega Blvd. to the Miracle Mile fashion mall that circles the property with 170 upscale chain stores and boutiques, dining venues such as **Trader Vic's** and a smattering of nightclubs. The casino is a large, roomy venue that has the Heart Bar at its center, a slick and clean-edged venue where a martini feels right. The casino also puts a novel Las Vegas stamp on gaming with the Pleasure Pit. From 8pm until the midnight hours the game is on and so is the dance, as go-go girls in scanty hot-wear rock it out on pedestals above the gaming tables. Dealers, too, put on their teddies and bustiers for the evening as the casino bets on players losing their shirts. Connected to Planet Hollywood is the **Westgate Tower** offering a residential condo experience, with floor to ceiling window seat areas, washer/dryer and kitchen, separate sleeping areas and its own lobby and pool area – all connected to the action of Planet Hollywood.

The Palms Casino Resort★

4321 W. Flamingo Rd.
702-942-7064 or 866-725-6773.
www.palms.com.
1,003 rooms. $$$

Built in 2001, this 55-story tower just off The Strip appeals to those who know the casino offers video-poker machines with some of the best odds in the city. At night, The Palms comes alive with pool parties at Skin, and late-night action at **Rain Nightclub** and **Ghost Bar** *(see Nightlife)*. The beds are famous, for comfort and size; "NBA rooms" accommodate the tallest of guests. In 2006 Palms opened the 40-story

Fantasy Tower with a series of suites geared to grab your attention. How about a suite with a bowling alley, or one with a full complement of basketball courts? If it can be dreamed up, the Palms will have it.

Stratosphere

2000 Las Vegas Blvd. S.
702-380-7777 or 800-998-6937.
www.stratlv.com.
2,444 rooms. $$

This property is the height of Vegas spectacular—its 1,149-foot **tower★** is the tallest freestanding structure west of the Mississippi. Test your fate on **Insanity** and be dangled over the edge of the tower, ride the **Big Shot** to be shot up its spire, or take the leap off the edge of the tower with **Skyjump Las Vegas**. In addition, there's a revolving restaurant in the needle, and two observation decks with great **views★★★**, so you can literally keep your nose in the air for hours. Check out Bite Las Vegas for an erotically-charged quest for the perfect specimen, or cool off at the roof top pool on the 8th floor.

Stratosphere

Las Vegas News Bureau

Flamingo Las Vegas

3555 Las Vegas Blvd. S.
702-733-3111 or 800-732-2111.
www.flamingolasvegas.com.
3,642 rooms. $$-$$$

The name Flamingo Hotel has survived from the 1940s era of Strip development, but in 1993 the Hilton Corporation razed the Flamingo's original motel-style buildings (created by gangster Bugsy Siegel), with its false stairways and bulletproof office. Today, the Flamingo comprises six towers of guest rooms, a wedding chapel, and a wildlife habitat. A top to bottom redo in 2006 and 2007 brought the "GO" room to the Flamingo, an Austin Powers-like pad of bubble gum pinks, sandy beiges and whites with bedside controls that move the drapes open and shut and lots of shiny plastic furniture details to put it all together. The pool is one of the lushest on The Strip, with waterfalls, wildlife and greenery.

Flamingo Las Vegas

Glenn Pinkerton/Las Vegas News Bureau

Tropicana Resort & Casino

3801 Las Vegas Blvd. S.
702-739-2222 or 800-634-4000.
www.tropicanalv.com.
1,800 rooms. $$-$$$

What's old is new again in Las Vegas, if it is not downed into rubble first. With a spiffy $125 million redo, the circa 1957 Tropicana Hotel was given a new Miami-themed persona and has reclaimed its title as "Tiffany of the Strip. The new South Beach style reaches into the pool areas where the 1960s trademark swim-up blackjack game remains amid waterfalls and lush landscaping, and the largest Nikki Beach location in the USA features a bar on a private island among other delights. The property is now home to the Las Vegas Mob Experience.

Rio Suites

3700 W. Flamingo Rd.
702-777-7777 or 888-746-7482.
www.playrio.com.
2,554 rooms. $$

Rio started the "suite" trend when it opened in 1990. Each "suite" is actually an oversized room with a large sofa area that can be used for sleeping. But the company got the jump on attractions when it opened its Masquerade in the Sky show over the casino area, which is a wonderfully creative mélange of New Orleans-style costumes and props with electric dancing and music. Sky floats allow guests to ride with the action once an hour above the casino floor. The hotel hosts parties at the Sapphire pool (admission charged), and adults only sessions at Lucky Strike Lanes.

MUST SEE

Pool area, Red Rock Resort

Station Casinos, Inc.

Red Rock Resort

1101 W. Charleston Blvd.
702-797-7777 or 866-767-7773.
www.redrocklasvegas.com.
460 rooms. $$-$$$

This resort marks the flagship for Station Casinos, a locals' fave known for great value dining, rooms and gaming odds. But this property brings the offerings to a new, top-quality level of hipness, handsome décor, spacious and comfortable rooms and action-packed scenes.
Crystal and rock is the theme here—and rock extends to outdoor concerts in the pool. A fabulous spa integrates the nearby desert into its programs.

Golden Nugget

129 E. Fremont St.
702-385-7111 or 800-634-3454.
www.goldennugget.com.
1907 rooms. $$

Downtown Las Vegas might just be the city's best-kept secret for fun and value; a stay at the Golden Nugget underscores this point. Suites here are huge and rent for the price of a small Strip hotel room. After a top to bottom $100-million redo in 2006 it has a cabana-lined pool with a three-story shark tank in the middle (and a see-through slide that tunnels right through it), new restaurants, a happening nightclub, a redone casino, and Downtown's only spa. For a modest fee you can have VIP check-in and concierge service.

The M Resort

12300 Las Vegas Blvd S.
702-797-1000 or 877-M-RESORT.
www.themresort.com.
390 Rooms. $$

M Resort is an odd apparition at the lonely junction of Las Vegas Boulevard and Blue Diamond Road at the far southern approach to the Strip. But space is also its appeal. Its 390 guestrooms are full of space at 550 square feet. The stand-alone property holds plenty of attraction in more than a dozen restaurants and bars: a hip wine room, a specialty brew bar, one of the best buffets in town attached to a culinary studio where guest chefs show and tell all. It also has a full service spa and a fashionable, but unintimidating pool.

CASINOS

GAMBLING

Oh, the games people play—blackjack, craps, keno, roulette, slot machines, and more. Gambling made the city what it is, and gambling remains its tour de force. Here are a few of the games of chance that gambling brings to the table (don't forget to tip your dealer):

Blackjack – The object is to draw cards that add up to 21 or as close to 21 as possible without going over that magic number. **Everybody at the table bets against the dealer.** If the dealer's first two cards total 16 or under, the dealer must "hit," or draw additional cards. If they add up to 17 or over, the dealer must stand. If the player's cards add up to more than the dealer's, but are under 21, the player wins. If the situation is reversed, the house wins (or they can tie and nobody wins). An ace and a face card or a ten together constitute blackjack, which automatically wins (except in the case of a tie).

Craps – On the first or "come out" roll in this fast-paced dice game, the "shooter" throws the dice to the other end of the table (dice must hit the wall of the table to be considered a legal roll). The shooter tries to establish a number—four, five, six, eight, nine or ten—then he tries to roll that number again before he rolls a seven.

Roulette – The roulette table is covered with 36 numbers plus a green zero and a green double zero (the European layout has only one zero). **Half of the 36 numbers are red and half are black.** Players may place chips on any combination of numbers. The winner is determined by where the marble-like ball comes to rest when the croupier spins the wheel. Players can wager on black or red,

> ### Who's Your Daddy?
> If slots or video poker is your game, sign up for the player's club; all casinos have them. These memberships allow you to accrue points as you play. The casino will reward your business with free restaurant vouchers, free play coupons, and maybe even a room. You'll get the house logo trucker's cap just for signing, and if you play enough, you'll be invited back—on the house.

even or odd, high or low, and even zero or double zero to enhance or complement their numbers or to get even odds on a spin. They can even put money on the corner or line of a number and split the risk among two or four numbers. But if a single number comes in with a wager squarely upon it, the pay out is 36 to one. Sweet!

Slots – These machines are as much about entertainment as they are about the jackpot. Nickel slots can still be found in most casinos. Quarters are more the standard, although you can play $1 to $500 in coin or token. Many machines taken on cartoon or movie themes and have an animated production that takes over for a bonus game if you make a certain combo in the roll. Players are advised to play all the lines—which usually means dropping nine or more coins for the maximum bet in each roll in order to keep the odds in their favor.

MUST SEE

To make the slots really pay off, join a players club. Then, simply insert the points card into the machine and watch the points add up with each play, win or lose. Points accrue quickly and come in handy for free buffet meals or dinners at the house gourmet room.

Baccarat – Baccarat calls for a tux and a 'tini, shaken—not stirred. It's considered a high-class card game because of high minimum bets waged in gold-plated rooms beneath glistening crystal.

But even if it was the preferred game for Bond, its dynamics are simple. Plus it offers some of the lowest house edges in the joint, allowing you to retrieve 99% of what you wager if you can hold out long enough. As with blackjack, two hands are dealt, and the higher hand wins. You can bet on either hand to win: the "Banker" or the "Player." Betting on the "Player" has a house edge of 1.24%, and betting on "Banker" has an edge of 1.06%. Even with the 5% commission added to a "Banker" win, it is still the best Baccarat play. Each player gets a turn to deal. Preset rules dictate whether a given hand can pull a third card, but three cards is the max, no matter what. The hand closer to nine wins. And unlike Blackjack, there's no such thing as a bust in Baccarat. Only the last digit of a two-card total over nine is counted (Ace is one, face is zero). Try to play at a crowded table for the best chance of holding on to your bankroll.

Video Poker – Slot lovers should take the video poker challenge for the best return for their time and money. It requires strategy and offers a decent chance to win good payoffs. The five coin max bet is recommended. The machine deals five cards, which can be kept or tossed by tapping the screen. Then you hit the DRAW button and you get replacement cards for the cards not kept. You win if you wind up with a poker hand of two pair, straight, flush, etc. Payouts depend on the style of machine played, and on its paytable, usually explained on top of the machine. Always wager the maximum as a sizable bonus reward is paid for a royal flush. Video poker offers some of the best odds in the casino, if a player plays well. Certain video poker machines have a return of over 100% with proper play, especially Deuces Wild, which pays up to 100.77%. You can find these machines downtown and in locals' casinos rather than The Strip.

Gaming in the pool, Caesars Palace

Glenn Pinkerton/Las Vegas News Bureau

VEGAS HEADLINERS

Frank Sinatra, Jerry Lewis, Dean Martin and Sammy Davis Jr. were among the names that took Vegas from a two-horse town to the entertainment capital of the world. When a star feels like playing it big, it means a Vegas tour, as Streisand did for her final official concerts, as Diana Ross did for her famous shows at Caesars, and as legends like Tony Bennett, Tom Jones and Elton John continue to do today. Although the headliner is steadily disappearing to an onslaught of production shows and the prolific creativity of Cirque du Soleil, there are still a few of these marquees blazing above the Vegas Strip. One of these is now Celine Dion.

Celine Dion

At Caesars Palace Colosseum. 3570 Las Vegas Blvd. S. celineinvegas.com. $55-$250 plus taxes and fees. 877-4CELINE (423-5463). Dark Mondays, Thursdays, Fridays.

Now, with Celine Dion in Las Vegas again, the city hopes it will be a new day. The star performer who packed the 4,300-seat Colosseum at Caesars for nearly five years straight is hoping she can do it again. The money at Caesars is on Celine Dion in Vegas as well. The trophy for the singer was securing a $100 million deal over the next three years – adding up to something like $20,000 a song.

When Dion left her previous run – A New Day with Cirque-like stage complements by Guy LaLiberte, the city of glamour was just beginning its recession-backed plunge, from which it is still reeling with losses topping $6 billion over the past three years. Dion went to a life of domestic bliss and newborn twins. But the show must go on. Celine Dion in Las Vegas could be worth $114 million a year to the city if the voice of diamonds and the touch of gold can still work its magic. "With the orchestra and the band we're going to be able to perform our songs like never before," Dion told fans before her March 2011 debut. "The repertoire is going be extraordinary...a mix of timeless

Celine Dion

© Gérard Schachmey/Caesars Entertainment

Great White Way West

Broadway has finally come to Las Vegas with such Tony-winning hits as **Jersey Boys** at Palazzo, **Phantom of the Opera** at The Venetian and **The Lion King** at Mandalay Bay. Soon, a new city concert hall, the Smith Performing Arts Center, will bring in true Broadway tours on a stage befitting the intent of live action musicals and drama. Meanwhile, Cirque du Soleil is busy opening its 7th Las Vegas show based on the hits of Michael Jackson in 2013.

Love at the Mirage, **Elvis** at Aria, **KÁ** at MGM Grand and the sexy **Zumanity** show at New York-New York continue to pull in the audiences. Le Rêve at Wynn uses a Cirque format of fancy aerial acts infused into a water-based arena of fire, rain and mist. At Luxor, Mindfreak's **Criss Angel** takes some tips from Cirque in his daring escapes and disappearances.

Hollywood classics, along with all the favorites that my fans like to hear me sing. It's going to be a very beautiful show, and I think we'll be raising the bar higher than we've ever done before. There'll be some truly wonderful moments."

Gone is the action and background glitz from the stage. The 90-minute show is all Celine, and her 31-piece Rat Pack-style band.

The five-time Grammy Award winner sings what people want to hear: *My Heart Will Go On* (Titanic, 1998), *Beauty and the Beast, It's All Coming Back to Me Now, Because You Loved Me...*

Dion's new show brings out her biggest hits and captures the romance of classic Hollywood movies performed with a stunning visual presentation. Visitors can make a night of it with VIP packages that score front row seats, among other treats. Dion will share the spotlight with fellow Canadian country superstar Shania Twain starting in December 2012. Twain's show, "Still the One," alternates with Dion and adds to a roster of three alternating megastar entertainers (including Rod Steward and Sir Elton John) who grace the stage of the Colosseum and cover the flashing Caesars Palace marquees when Dion is not playing.

Barry Manilow

At Paris Las Vegas. 3655 Las Vegas Blvd. S. 702-946-7000 or 888-266-5687. www.manilowparis.com

Barry Manilow spent a good chunk of his time telling fans that if they wanted to see him perform, they would have to come to his house. Happily for his fans, Manilow had a home at the 1,700-seat Hilton Theater in the Las Vegas. He has now moved to the Paris Theater at Paris Las Vegas where he performs Friday, Saturday and Sunday nights.

Denise Truscello/Caesars Entertainment

Barry Manilow

Well into his 60s the balladeer shows no signs of slowing down. After more than three decades of performing and a career that has produced more than 50 albums, Manilow performs with all the gusto of his younger years, dutifully dusting off such hits as "Mandy," "It's a Miracle," "Could It Be Magic?" "I Write the Songs," and "Copacabana." He also throws in some pop numbers mixing high-tech sounds with the Las Vegas classics once performed by Frank Sinatra, Elvis Presley, Sammy Davis Jr., and Dean Martin.

Barry, Bette Midler's former pianist and musical director, admits that his strength lies in musical arrangements; "I'm a fair singer, I write nice songs, but I'm a great arranger," he has admitted. "My songs are like anchovies. Some people love them, some people get nauseous." So far, he has sold more than 60 million records.

Rita Rudner

At The Venetian, 3355 Las Vegas Blvd. S. 702-414-1000 or 866-641-7469. www.ritafunny.com. Performances run Mondays and Wednesdays at 8:30 pm and Saturdays at 6 pm.

This lady of Las Vegas has done it all: MGM, New York New York, Harrah's, … and now The Venetian with an unflagging sense of humor that still sticks you right in the ribs. Comedienne Rita Rudner running *Now Funny* at her new home in the Venetian Showroom has yet to run out of ways to attach droll comedy to the oddity of every day life – from her marriage to writer/producer Martin Bergman to the trials and triumphs of life with her adopted daughter, Molly, and whatever can go wrong with pet canine, Bonkers (named after her grandfather). Rita works like a dog during each of her stage shows, as she unleashes her talents on a waiting world who knows more about her life sometimes than they do their own.

Rita Rudner

The Venetian

MUST SEE

PRODUCTIONS
QUINTESSENTIAL VEGAS

One of the attributes of Las Vegas that puts a feather in the city's cap was the Las Vegas showgirl. With her plumed headdresses and long legs, she and the lavish productions in which she appeared became synonymous with the city in its early years. Alas, the day of the Vegas showgirl is gone, replaced by flashier productions that appeal to a more sophisticated audience with higher-tech tastes in risqué productions. Still, if you hanker for good old-fashioned entertainment, this Las Vegas survivor takes the cake – and the Titanic, too … Topless.

🌿 Donn Arden's Jubilee!

At Bally's Las Vegas, 3645 Las Vegas Blvd. S. 800-237-7469. www.ballyslv.com. (Late show at 10:30pm is topless.)

Caesars Entertainment

It may have modern-day costumes, sets, sound, lights, choreography and a nearly 100-member cast, but Jubilee! is still a throwback to Las Vegas' Golden Age of lavish stage spectaculars. Having celebrated its 30th anniversary in 2011, Jubilee! is the second longest-running Lido show on the Strip (trailing Folies Bergere at the Tropicana, which finally closed the curtain in 2009 after 49 years). The quintessential Vegas-style revue was conceived by the late Donn Arden, best known for introducing the Lido de Paris— and the topless showgirl—to the city in the mid-1950s.

When it premiered in 1981 at what was then the MGM Grand, Jubilee! was bigger and more spectacular than any other show on The Strip. The original staging of Jubilee! cost $10 million. More than 1,000 costumes are worn during the show, many of them designed by world-renowned designers Bob Mackie and Pete Menefee. Based on Jerry Herman's Hundreds of Girls, the opening act features

76 performers in feathered headdresses. In the Ziegfeld Follies-style ending, the cast, walks down a staircase to the tune of "A Pretty Girl Is Like a Melody"—a Vegas classic. The show ends with a bang as the stage turns into the Titanic.

Fun Facts

A hundred different sets require some 100,000 light bulbs and over 125 miles of wiring; 4,200lbs of dry ice are used each week; 10lbs of explosives burst nightly in 50 pyrotechnic effects; during the iceberg scene in the "Titanic" number, 5,000 gallons of recycled water cascade across the stage; 8,000 miles of sequins, two tons of feathers and 10,000 pounds of jewelry are used; the heaviest feathered headdress weighs 35lbs —the heaviest hat? 20lbs.

CIRQUE DU SOLEIL

This extraordinary troupe started as a group of street performers in Baie-Saint-Paul, Quebec, in 1982. The company now has almost 4,000 employees from over 40 different countries, including more than 1,000 artists. Cirque du Soleil currently has six shows in Vegas … and counting. Cirque is also the creative influence behind the Revolution Lounge at the Mirage, its first foray into spheres beyond pure performance. However, the circus is always its center stage, and to keep its productions stocked with the world's top triple jointed talents, Las Vegas has a circus school, one of the few in the US. On any given day one can find Cirque performers and Cirque hopefuls dangling and dancing on lines of silk from a 50-foot ceiling, or balancing on a rope closer to the ground. Injuries on stage are not uncommon. Once in the Cirque, it is a life-long commitment, whether as a performer finding impossible ways to move muscles, or as a teacher.

Mystère

At Treasure Island, 3300 Las Vegas Blvd. S. 800-392-1999. www.treasureisland.com.

Hoping to find real treasure at Treasure Island? It comes in the form of performance without boundaries, ballet without gravity and theater without actors. It's Mystère: a surrealistic celebration of music, dance, acrobatics and comedy from the artistic body that holds the patent on imagination-

bending—Cirque du Soleil. Although the 72-odd member cast incorporates basic circus concepts in their productions, any similarity to any circus you have ever seen before ends there. Relying on the performers and their limitless creativity, Mystère presents stunning feats on the trapeze, Korean plank, and Chinese poles, as well as an aerial bungee ballet.

"O"

At Bellagio, 3600 Las Vegas Blvd. S. 888-488-7111 or 702-693-7722. www.bellagio.com.

The star of this Cirque du Soleil spectacle (at Bellagio for an indefinite run) is 1.5 million gallons of water, representing the circle of life. With this mesmerizing show, the troupe ventures for the first time into aquatic theater, wherein Cirque du Soleil reaches fascinating new heights. From the moment the curtain parts to reveal a forest-like setting on stage, the mysteries of "O" begin to unfold. Floors disappear into pools of water and walls vanish in the mist. The cast of 74 synchronized swimmers,

Mystère

Al Seib/Cirque du Soleil

divers, contortionists and trapeze artists perform incredible feats in and over this liquid stage, which transforms itself from one body of water to another in the space of a few seconds.

KÀ

At MGM Grand, 3799 Las Vegas Blvd. S. 702-891-1111 or 877-264-1845. www.ka.com.

Just when you thought Cirque du Soleil could not possibly dream up another amazing theater-of-the-bizarre production, along comes KÀ, which may well be their best endeavor to date. Named after an Egyptian word for the invisible spirit duplicate of the body that accompanies each person throughout this life and into the next, KÀ blends fire and special effects with riveting results. Eighty athletic performers infuse martial arts, acrobatics, puppetry, interactive video and pyrotechnics to support a plot that spotlights imperial twins (a boy and girl) who take off on a danger-laden adventure that separates their fates and ultimately reunites them. The tale moves through 27 haunting sequences of purifying and destructive fire, dreamscapes of storms and floods, tender moments of shadow puppetry, and precipitous battle scenes staged on an impossibly tilted stage, which at one point, rotates—with the performers on it—a full 360 degrees.

Humorous encounters with gigantic sand-dwelling crustaceans add to the fun. The Cirque's signature bungee props and swing poles are featured in ethereal numbers, all enhanced by an extraordinary score of chorus and orchestra.

Love

At The Mirage, 3400 Las Vegas Blvd. S. 702-791-7111 or 800-963-9634. www.thebeatleslove.com.

The Cirque opened the Beatles-themed production inside a 360-degree custom-created theater at the Mirage in 2006 using the master tapes at Abbey Road Studios to create a multi-sensory Beatles experience that is as dazzling to watch as it is to hear. Employing film projections of the Fab Four as a backdrop against a dazzling continuum of impossible choreography, mesmerizing special effects, and riveting costume and inventive stage design, the show marks the fist time in the Cirque's two dozen years that actual lyrics are integral to the music. The show and music is everywhere through, at some counts, 6,000 speakers including those built into each and every seat. "Love" was all that was needed to fulfil an aspiration inspired by the friendship between George Harrison and Cirque director Gilles Ste-Croix. The results are stunning. You've never heard the Beatles like this.

Zumanity

At New York-New York, 3970 Las Vegas Blvd. S. 702-740-6969. www.zumanity.com.

Nudity is just another costume in this sexy Cirque du Soleil show where acrobatics, languid ballet moves, and amazing feats of human physicality produce one wow after another. It's performed in the style of European cabaret

PRODUCTIONS

theater in acts with names like "2Men" and "Gentle Orgy"—get the picture?

🎸 Viva Elvis

Elvis Theater at Aria. 3730 Las Vegas Blvd. S. 702-590-7760. www.arialasvegas.com.

It's been nearly 50 years since Elvis disappeared from the marquee at the Las Vegas Hilton for better times in a world beyond. But sightings aside you are more likely to encounter the ghost of Elvis's ghost today than anything resembling The King in all his heft and charisma. Common are heavily side-burned, well-wigged impersonators who come out for events and regular stroll downtown's Fremont Street at night greeting tourists under the VivaVision canopy and posing for snapshots. Sure, Elvis can still be found officiating weddings around town. Of the best places to see Elvis, however, is at Viva Elvis, the new Cirque de Soleil show at Aria. The 90-minute Elvis Show is full of energy, zip, creative staging and wonderful Elvis music that starts at his earliest musical mentions and moves through his life. It's a tribute show that uses authentic film footage as a backdrop. The rare footage complements colorful Cirque performances that run from sock-hopping girls in poodle skirts and pageboys to musical stagings of his going off to Viet Nam to ethereal numbers involving acrobatics and aerial flight maneuvers around a giant Gibson guitar.

If you want to hear Elvis numbers that rock you to the core, the sound system at the new theater at Aria makes that happen through such numbers at Blue Suede Shoes, Don't Be Cruel, One Night with You, All Shook Up, Saved, Got a lot of Lovin' to Do, Return to Sender, Viva Las Vegas and Jailhouse Rock. There are around a dozen numbers set to life on stage and, unlike the stage at LOVE, the Cirque's Beatle's tribute playing at the Mirage, the stage here is not a stage in the round but a formal platform, making it easier to stay focused on the exquisite performances. Still, Elvis remains larger than life through it all and with the chronological element in place even those people who have never set eyes on the guy will come away with a true appreciation of his talents.

Without a doubt, Viva Elvis is the best place to see Elvis while you are in town. Sightings are guaranteed and tickets start at $116.40 and counting. Dinner and show packages are available that allow you to make a whole evening out of it.

For instance, one of the best places to see Elvis with dinner is Julian Serrano, an eponymous restaurant by the acclaimed two-star Michelin chef, which specializes in refined Spanish cuisine and tapas. Show your ticket and get the dinner: a three-course prix fixe menu for $45 per person. Performances run 7 and 9:30 nightly, except Tuesday and Wednesday.

MUST SEE

VEGAS FAVORITES

Nowhere is Las Vegas' "wow" factor more apparent than in its production shows. Here are a few of our favorites.

Jersey Boys

Isaac Brekken/The Palazzo

Jersey Boys

The Palazzo. 3325 Las Vegas Blvd. S. 702-414-9000 or 877-883-6423. www.jerseyboysinfo.com/vegas.

Before Franki Valli got wacked as a dufus bad-boy character on HBO's The Sopranos, he had a life as a season – one of the Four Seasons who set the '60s aglow with such hits as "Sherry," "Dawn" and "Walk Like a Man."

The Jersey Boys, straight from Broadway, has been setting the Vegas entertainment platform alight since it opened in 2008 at the Palazzo as a permanent fixture that has just rounded three years. The storyline follows four blue-collar kids working their way from the streets of Newark to the heights of stardom. But for all its predictability it also predictably draws the audience in, sends them on a rocketing crescendo of favorite retro tunes and lets them down with an aftertaste of pure sweetness. The show unfolds daily,

except Mondays. Do expect to find yourself rattling off Walk Like a Man and Can't Take My Eyes off of You days later at a stoplight or when fumbling through the mail. The show definitely gets under your skin. CDs and souvenirs are in the adjacent gift shop. Performances run daily except Wednesday starting at $72.10.

Absinthe

The Spiegeltent at Caesars Palace. 3570 Las Vegas Blvd. S. 800-745-3000. www.absinthevegas.com.

Caesars Entertainment

Absinthe

PRODUCTIONS

It's been described as Cirque du Soleil channeled through Rocky Horror Picture Show. Absinthe, Las Vegas is the latest spectacular to grace the Las Vegas Strip -- an adult carnival that transforms the Roman Plaza in front of Caesars Palace into an entertainment playground under a big top.

Within a maze of tents and early 20th Century European decor this Las Vegas show is actually an adult carnival of immersion experiences, complete with a secret speakeasy, raucous beer garden and mischievous drinking games. As evening approaches, the Absinthe performances begin starting at 7:30 pm Tuesday through Sunday. Especially stunning is the heritage wooden show tent from Europe opulently decorated with mirrors, stained glass and velvet and surrounding the audience in a theatre-in-the-round presentation. The ringleader of Absinthe and its carnival of crazed characters is a one of a kind called Gazillionaire, who leads the close-up audience of 600 people down a decadence-laced and fun-fueled evening of extraordinary performances. The costumes, the impossible contortions and the fantastical illusions are all part of the rapture. The Gazillionaire brings out his most outrageous friends, his exotic family and even some deranged servants to entertain and mesmerize crowds in this 90-minute frenzy of performances. Among the characters is his loyal assistant Penny, "The Green Fairy," his butler Max, "The Weather Girl," "Duo Ssens," "The Skating Aratas" and "The Esteemed Gentlemen of the High Wire."

As one observer described it, "Absinthe is a hallucination. You enter the Salon Marlene Spiegeltent, which is like stepping aboard a 100-year-old carousel, and journeying back to the Moulin Rouge in 1909." A "Cirque on Acid?" Or perhaps on a century old bottle of Absinthe with the dangerous wormwood left in tact.

Absinthe has had successful runs in both New York and Miami and is gambling that Vegas will provide a popular and, perhaps, permanent home for its band of outcasts and their clever stunts.

Blue Man Group

MUST SEE

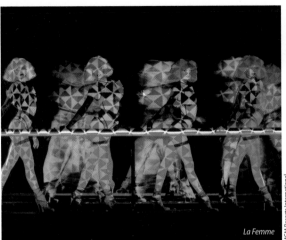

La Femme

MGM Resorts International

🎭 Blue Man Group

At The Venetian, 3355 Las Vegas Blvd. S. 702-414-1000 or 888-283-6423. www.blueman.com.

If you haven't seen Blue Man Group, by all means, do. In 2005 the unique blue-hued trio moved from Luxor, where the show had been playing since March 2000, to a 1,750-seat theater built just for them at the Venetian. Surprises galore await audiences already mesmerized by drum beats and syncopated colors enhanced by tubes, shadows and effects. The show can be seen again and again as no two are the same.

🎭 La Femme

At MGM Grand, 3799 Las Vegas Blvd. S. 702-891-7777. www.mgmgrand.com.

Straight from the Crazy Horse in Paris, this intimate feminine revue celebrates women in a way that Americans rarely do. The stage fills

with 13 dancers, chosen for their lithe bodies, flexibility and ability to turn on the energy with just a smile. Sparse costuming gives way to elaborate stage props and engaging musical performances on the small stage.

All seats here are good ones and put the audience right up to the action—a rare experience in a town where most performances are watched from a distance. Spots for the troupe here are very competitive. Dancers often hail from Russian ballet academies and lives of strict classical training.

🎭 Le Rêve

Wynn Las Vegas, 3131 Las Vegas Blvd. S. 702-770-9966 or 888-320-7110. www.wynnlasvegas.com.

Opened in 2005, Le Rêve (French for "the dream") plays in the Wynn Theater, a 2,087-seat theater in the round. The show immerses 75 Cirque-du-Soleil-trained artists into a watery stage for 90 minutes

PRODUCTIONS

51

Le Rêve

© Tomasz Rossa/Wynn Las Vegas

of glorious dream sequences. This work is the achievement of Franco Dragone, former director of Cirque du Soleil. As in a dream, the haunting sequences meld together and the message is what you make it. If you sit in the first three rows of any section, prepare to get soaked (the staff passes out towels before the show).

Phantom of the Opera

Isaac Brekken/The Venetian

🎭 Phantom of the Opera

At The Venetian, 3355 Las Vegas Blvd. 702-414-9000 or 877-883-6423. www.phantomlasvegas.com.

Phantom never seems to go out of style. See it once, see it two dozen times, it still delights the soul and rivets the imagination no matter how many times you have seen the chandelier drop. See it in Vegas, however, and see it anew. First, the show has been fine-tuned for the standard 90-minute Vegas format. Second, the show plays in a custom-built theater designed with the greatest of care to give the illusion that you are actually in the Paris Opera House.

Third, the staging employs a variety of impressive special effects and fourth—audiences have the rare, if not exceptional, opportunity to take a stage tour and go backstage to meet the cast—including the Phantom, unmasked.

MUST SEE

AFTERNOON SHOWS

Las Vegas has always been looked upon as a late-night town. But the fun of an afternoon show can never be overrated. This is both old Vegas and new at its finest and usually for the right price. Please note: while the weather may not change much in Las Vegas, shows do.

Mac King

At Harrah's, 3475 Las Vegas Blvd. S. 702-369-5111, ext. 5222. www.mackingshow.com/las-vegas.

If comedy-magic is your bag, then the Mac King Show, appearing afternoons in the Improv theater at Harrah's, is something you won't want to miss. King's unique act is not your run-of-the-mill magic show; it contains an unusual combination of quirky humor, visual gags, and amazing sleights of hand. Delivered in an hilarious tongue-in-cheek manner, it's serious magic.

Besides making his head disappear inside a paper bag, King fishes live goldfish out of the air, finds an audience member's playing card in a sealed box of cereal, transforms himself into Siegfried & Roy and then transforms Siegfried & Roy into a white tiger. Of course, the

audience is invited to participate. After the show, you can find King outside selling T-shirts and chatting with his fans.

King is known for his engaging personality and original illusions. Among them is his infamous Cloak of Invisibility, an ordinary yellow raincoat that possesses "extraordinary" powers.

King's Credits

King has appeared on seven NBC magic specials and holds the distinction of being the only performer to have performed on all five of NBC's *World's Greatest Magic* shows. He was most recently seen on the Late Show with David Letterman in 2008, and on Fox receiving an award for Best Comedy Magician at the 2007 World Magic Awards hosted by Sir Roger Moore.

Caesars Entertainment

Mac King

PRODUCTIONS

53

King convinces the audience that this coat renders him invisible. The hilarious gag that follows involves astounding illusory feats.

The comedic magician also tosses his cookies—Fig Newtons—between the magical states of "now you see them" and "now you don't." King's affinity for Fig Newtons is a recurring sight gag in the show; the cookies seem to appear in the most unlikely places throughout his performance and disappear in the same manner—into his mouth or the mouths of audience members.

The Price is Right – Live!

At Bally's, 3645 Las Vegas Blvd. S.
800-237-7469 or 702-967-4567
www.ballyslasvegas.com.
Dark Sundays, Mondays.
Plays Friday at 7:30 pm;
All other days, 2:30 pm.

Take an icon of American television history, put it on the Las Vegas stage and you are bound to get it right—in this case "The Price is Right."

It's live. It's got the wit, the pace, and the prizes. What it does not

Show and Tell

Love that TV screen? **Television City** at the MGM Grand wants you. It runs hourly screenings each day from 10am to 8:30pm to get viewer response to an array of primetime shows in the pipeline at CBS and other networks. Screenings are free, take place in four viewing rooms and give serious weight to audience reaction. Participants should be at least 14 years old.

have is the camera and Bob Barker. But Todd Newton, famed face from *E! News Live* and *Coming Attractions*, keeps the show going with jokes and gags and models to make it pretty.

Aficionados of the show will recognize the pricing games: Cliff Hangers, Clock Game, Hole in One, Race Game, Plinko, It's in the Bag, and the Big Wheel, as contestants "come on down" and guess what common American consumer items cost. Prizes range from luggage to appliances to that "brand new car"! Audience members must be

The Price is Right – Live!

Caesars Entertainment

MUST SEE

21 years old to be a contestant, pay the $49.50 admission and register at a booth located by the theater up to three hours before the show. Each of the 50 registrants receives a yellow price tag with their name. Players are chosen randomly for each round. Other audience members win Harrah's player points and other small prizes during the show.

The thrills last 105 minutes, but for the lucky few they may last much longer.

Nathan Burton Comedy Magic

At Flamingo Hotel and Casino, 3555 Las Vegas Blvd. S. 702-733-3333 or 888-902-9929. www.harrahs.com; www.nathanburton.com.

Nathan Burton brings afternoons to life in the Flamingo Showroom with his comedic ensemble of magic feats. Burton has been performing magic since the age of 4, but has managed to hone his act into a 60-minute whirlwind of in-your-face magical stunts blended with humor and, of course, showgirls. He received national attention recently when he took on the Ultimate Las Vegas Showgirl Challenge (2008) by spending seven nights inside a sealed box with seven showgirls—a stunt that received national attention from E! Entertainment and CNN's Larry King. He also won a good deal of attention for the Miracle Mile Shops at Planet Hollywood Resort when he encased himself in a gigantic M-shaped ice sculpture in front of the mall on the Las Vegas Strip, joined by a rotating cast of bikini-clad showgirls inside the nine tons of ice. Visitors cruising The Strip could touch and inspect the 'M' and join in on the improbable occasion. His show makes for an excellent midday diversion, at the "lost hour" of 4pm, as a warm up for a wild evening ahead.

Piano! Las Vegas

V Theater in the Miracle Mile. 3663 Las Vegas Blvd. S. 702-260-7200 or 866-932-1818. www.pianolasvegas.com.

It's easy to find comfort on a hot afternoon in Las Vegas, especially if you beat the heat with a comedic maestro like Ryan Ahern. The guy does Broadway to Rock 'n Roll making the keys on the piano seem more like a handy deck of cards than a refined classical instrument. Ahern simply pushes out the notes with the simplicity of a shuffle and yet through all the complexity and speed does not miss a beat with his jokes and singing.

He's backed by band of six who keep the arrangements flowing. The range runs contemporary to classic with medleys such as Maroon Five's This Love and Seal's Kiss From a Rose, to favorite hits including Ray Charles' Mess Around, Jerry Lee Lewis' Great Balls of Fire and Queen's Bohemian Rhapsody to John Williams' Theme from E.T. to Bette Midler's Wind Beneath My Wings and the staccato meanderings of Malaguena and Flight of the Bumblebee.

The theater is in the Miracle Mile Shops at Planet Hollywood. *Tickets start at $29.99. Performances happen at 2:30 pm Saturdays through Thursdays.*

PRODUCTIONS

MAGIC SHOWS

Now you see them … now you see them again and again and again. Las Vegas' resident headliner magicians have something up their sleeves indeed—tigers, women, birds, rocket ships and knives, to name a few. Faster than speeding bullets, able to leap tall reputations in a single bound, they are the supermen of the magic scene.

Amazing Johnathan

At Planet Hollywood in the Harmon Theater, 3667 Las Vegas Blvd. S. 702-785-5555 or 866-919-PHRC (7472). www.amazingj.com.

Seeing is believing, and nowhere is that truer than at Planet Hollywood, where the Amazing Johnathan appears every night but Wednesday and Thursday. From the moment the comedic magician walks out on stage, he offers a crystal-clear picture of bizarre comedy—while calmly gulping down Windex at any given moment. With his bonafide don't-try-this-at-home act billed as "where magic and comedy collide," Johnathan focuses his impact on getting laughs. Nightly packed houses watch Johnathan eat razor

It's Amazing

There are two real magic tricks in the Amazing Johnathan's show—the rest is spoof. Each of his shows is preceded by interactive audience comedy (via a live video camera and a *big* screen) and a different comedy or magic opening act weekly. During each show, Johnathan always brings up a "willing" participant on stage to assist him.

Parents beware: Johnathan does use profanity in his performance.

blades, put a knife through his arm, put a pencil in his ear and out his nose, and swig Windex. Now, even without the help of his trusty assistant, the Psychic Tanya, Johnathan himself can see clearly into the future. And he's going to keep people laughing for a long time to come.

By his own admission, the acclaimed performer is as edgy and as politically incorrect as he can be. But he emphasizes that it's all in jest; he doesn't cross the line from funny to mean-spirited. His fast, furious and extremely funny approach has earned him rave reviews. Rolling Stone magazine refers to him as "one of the best comics working today." Among his honors, he is a two-time winner of the International Magic Award for "Best Comedy Magician."

Amazing Johnathan

Preferred Public Relations & Marketing

MUST SEE

Criss Angel: Believe

© APWI Photographer: Matthew Burke/Cirque du Soleil

Criss Angel: Believe

Believe Theater at Luxor.
3900 Las Vegas Blvd. S.
702-262-4400 or 800-288-1000.
www.crissangel.com/believe.

The man who has captivated audiences through six seasons so far of Mindfreak on the Arts & Entertainment channel, packs a hall of fresh faces Tuesday to Saturday – a good lot of them 8 year olds who want to grow up to be just like him. That level of audience appreciation sets the stage for some heady, albeit expensive, entertainment that will wow the wildest child. Adults, however, might want to use to the time to up their skill level on Free Birds through much of the performance.

While Las Vegas is a tough town to be a magician – audiences have seen it all before – you have to pull something super strange and novel out of your hat to keep your name on the marquee. For Angel, that something else was Cirque du Soleil. The magician and the Cirque's creative team collaborated for months to create a show that would be the perfect intersection of master trickery with all the layers of Goth and fantasy a Cirque set could deliver.

But since its opening in 2008, any shadow of Cirque involvement is mostly gone, save a sexy blonde assistant in occasionally stunning costumes. The rest is heavy-handed, rough hewn, but implicitly sensitive Criss and his repertoire of tricks. Most of those tricks focus on disappearing into boxes, seats, walls and reappearing in some other improbably location.

Still, the actor is talented and handsome and has a loyal television audience. And he comes up with tricks, if not amazing new stunts, every couple of weeks. But if you are expecting Alice in Wonderland meets Houdini in Vegas, might as well stick to books.

MAGIC SHOWS

57

♣ Penn & Teller

At Rio, 700 W. Flamingo Rd.
702-777-7777 or 888-746-7784.
www.pennandteller.com.

The bad boys of magic, Penn & Teller always strive to make their audiences feel at home. That's because for this magical duo, home is where the wood chipper, handcuffs, razor blades, guns, and other props of their act are—it's wise to stay awake for this one! Luckily, home for Penn & Teller is at the Rio these days, where their act has become a permanent fixture (*nightly except Friday*), and the hotel happily cleans up the blood. The duo refers to themselves as "a couple of eccentric guys who have learned how to do a few cool things." *Newsweek* magazine described them as "pure entertainment and demented originality"; *Entertainment Weekly* dubbed them "two of the funniest people alive"; and David Letterman referred to the pair as "evil geniuses." However you view it, what you see is what you get with these two. Together since 1975, Penn & Teller are so-called "swindlers and scam artists" who

Penned and Teller-All

Penn & Teller have penned three best-selling books, *Cruel Tricks for Dear Friends, How to Play with Your Food* and *How to Play In Traffic.* They also have a popular series on the Showtime network.

perform tricks (and scams) with rather threatening props, not to mention the occasional bunny in a wood chipper. Their unique brand of magic and bizarre comedy includes throwing knives at attractive females in the audience, eating fire with a showgirl, transforming a wayward girl into an 800-pound gorilla; and hanging Penn by the neck while Teller does hand shadows. Vegas audiences force the pair to keep sharpening up their old tricks and coming up with new, more spectacular stunts. One can only imagine….
Teller's silent, creepy magic, mixed with Penn's clown and juggling expertise have taken the performers from street theater to international fame and this regular slot at the Rio All-Suite Hotel & Casino.

Penn & Teller

Penn & Teller

MUST SEE

Dirk Arthur's Wild Magic

O'Shea's Theater, 3555 Las Vegas Blvd. S. 702-733-3333

Dirk Arthur performs some wild magic in his nightly performances at O'Shea's Las Vegas. And it's because of those wild stunts that the show is truly a show. Arthur is a prop magician, relying on elaborate props and showmanship for the real thrust of his magical entertainment.

The props do not get better than this: Bengal tigers, white-striped tigers, a pure white snow tiger, and black African leopards. He makes these man-eaters appear and disappear with the ease of a passing hand.

An authentic 26-foot long Robinson helicopter also materializes out of the blue.

Las Vegas is well known for its array of prop magician shows—Siegfried & Roy, David Copperfield—it takes a big stage and a lot of work to create these illusions. Naturally, there are showgirls and dancers and a variety of talents moving through the show, which runs twice daily, except Monday.

Dirk Arthur Wild Magic

Caesars Entertainment

David Copperfield

At MGM Grand, 3799 Las Vegas Blvd. S 702-891-7777 or 877-880-0880. www.dcopperfield.com

Master magician David Copperfield is a magician's magician who is well known for his amazing stunts, such as making the Statue of Liberty disappear. In his ongoing engagements at MGM Grand's Hollywood Theater he does not back down from his signature antics. For instance, rather than

causing a great American icon to vanish, he turns the trick on himself, making himself disappear, reappear and his assistants do the same. As with his ghost-like walk through the Great Wall of China, he takes the feat to the stage by seeming to penetrate a solid block of metal.

Copperfield's hard-won illusions are grand enough to have earned him 21 television specials through the years. He has a place in the Guinness Book of World Records, nearly two dozen Emmys, even a star on Hollywood's Walk of Fame. In Las Vegas his act includes such odd feats as the magician transporting himself and a member of the audience from the stage to a deserted island on the other side of the planet.

At other times he makes whole swaths of the audience disappear. Plenty of audience participation is involved in this fast-paced and electrifying show.

GREAT IMPOSTERS

Some of Las Vegas' favorite performers just aren't themselves these days—everyone from Elvis to Neil Diamond to Kermit the Frog. These personalities suddenly have a doppelganger in the repertoire of the great impressionists—such as 🎭 Danny Gans—who play Las Vegas. That's good news for nightlife.

🎭 Barbra and Frank, The Concert That Never Was

At the Westin Casuarina. 60 East Flamingo Road. 702-836-5900. www.barbraandfrank.com

Las Vegas may be known for its super-sized resorts and its over-the-top faux architecture and attractions, but it's also the world's epicenter for celebrity imposter acts. One must-see example is Barbra and Frank, The Concert That Never Was, at the Riviera's Le Bistro Lounge.

The mismatched duo of Sharon Owens and Sebastian Anzaldo make something that might never have worked—a concert featuring Barbra Streisand and Frank Sinatra—into a good show, with some hokey comedic numbers

and lots of good crooning. The moody, cigarette-toting chairman indulging in witty repartee with the motor-mouthed heroine of *Funny Girl* is in itself an act to behold, and it's made ever more charming with the lineup of sentimental songs and fine piano accompaniment. The tribute opens with both performers singing "I've Got A Crush On You" à la the 1993 Duets album. They depart into solos and return again for more banter at the piano, lapsing into such tunes as "Witchcraft," "Bewitched, Bothered and Bewildered," "You Don't Bring Me Flowers" and build up to the "New York, New York" crescendo. Among Frank's solo numbers are "I've Got The World On A String," "Summer Wind," "Come Fly With Me," "Fly Me To The Moon," and "My Way."

Barbra and Frank, The Concert That Never Was

Terry Factor

Anzaldo as Sinatra brings the audience to their feet with a moving rendition of "That's Life."

🎵 Terry Fator: Ventriloquism in Concert

Terry Fator Theater at The Mirage. 3400 Las Vegas Blvd. S. 702-792-7777 or 800-627-6667. www.terryfator.com.

When Las Vegas star, Danny Gans, died in 2009, the king of comedy impersonations left a huge hole in the talent fabric of the Las Vegas Strip. Las Vegas star marketers knew it would take some big talent to fill that microphone and make a successful run at The Mirage. The showroom was built for Gans and was his show home for a dozen years.

But if Las Vegas has anything, it's got talent. Straight into those shoes walked less known Las Vegas star Terry Fator: a puppeteer, ventriloquist and celebrity impersonator who won the big one on "America's Got Talent." As he says in his own words, "It only took me 32 years to become an overnight

sensation." And now on stage at Mirage that sensation has settled into a permanent new spot along the corridor of top Strip marquees. A true student of the voice-throwing greats before him, Fator takes the talents of Edgar Bergen, Buffalo Bob Smith, Shari Lewis, Wayland Flowers and Jim Henson and mixes in the pipes of Garth Brooks, Rod Stewart, Etta James, Louie Armstrong, Axl Rose, Michael Jackson, even Ozzie Osbourne and, of course, Elvis.

In fact, it was his riveting "At Last" by Etta James – set to a cute character of a puppet named Emma – that snatched the $1 million television talent show prize

Terry Fator was the $1 million winner of the televised **"America's Got Talent"** contest in 2007, and has been called "one of the most talented people on the planet" by Simon Cowell himself. He channels Garth Brooks, Rod Stewart, Etta James, Louie Armstrong, Axl Rose and, inevitably, Elvis – and often all inside a five minute yodel.

GREAT IMPOSTERS

Frankly Speaking

Marino gets some of his material from some very unique sources. When it comes to the designs for his gowns, 90 percent of the time he dreams up the ideas and the rest come from some offbeat sources. One of those places is from the Barbie doll, which the impersonator claims has the best fantasy dresses. Marino quips that he is actually a copy of Barbie, "the only one who has more plastic parts than him."

and which anchors his nightly show and blows away the audience each time.

Fator plays the clueless straight guy to a series of mop-top, mean-faced, oatmeal-brained, sexy, savvy and silly puppet characters he fondly refers to as his "guests." Topping the list is Winston the Impersonating Turtle (think Kermit with a carapace), then there is

> **Frank Marino** has been voted "Best Dressed in Las Vegas" repeatedly. It's no wonder with what he has to choose from:
> ♦ 2,000 evening gowns
> ♦ A trunk full of jewelry
> ♦ 50 wigs
> ♦ 300 pairs of shoes

Wayland Jennings wannabe, Walter T. Airdale, the voluptuous Vikki the "cougar," rocker-stoner Dougie, jive talking and soul-singing Julius, and Maynard Tomkins the Elvis guy who doesn't know any Elvis songs.

From these characters come the impressive sounds of celebrity singers from voice throwing Fator who, without moving his mouth, has been described as a "human i-Pod." He moves seamlessly from one character to the next, one song to the next, one act to the next through a river of distinct voices and sounds, all his own.

The show is as much a testimony to what humans are capable of as it is a platform of entertaining, amusing and often riveting human talent – American style.

Frank Marino's Diva Las Vegas

MUST SEE

Diva Las Vegas

Imperial Palace. 3535 Las Vegas Blvd. S. www.imperialpalace.com. 702-731-3311 or 800-634-6441. Nightly, except Fridays, at 10 pm.

It's not easy being She, especially if that woman is Frank Marino as more than a half dozen superwomen in a 75-minute comedy and song-filled show. Marino might be considered Las Vegas' original diva, most famous for channeling the spirit of Joan Rivers, gowns, face-lifts and all, and running hilarious monologues in her voice. After 25 years at La Cage at the Riviera, however, Marino went solo, with his ladies in tow, and has not looked back.

Diva Las Vegas brings on the stars from Britney Spears to Cher, to Diana Ross to Beyonce, and not forgetting Madonna, Dolly Parton and, of course, Pop's newest sensation Lady Gaga. Marino changes his Bob Mackie gowns and towering Manolo Blahnik between characters in a show, which stars, Joan Rivers, naturally.

Marino has become a Las Vegas icon in his own right and so much a part of the city fabric that Mayor Oscar Goodman tabbed February 1 to be Frank Marino Day.

 Gordie Brown

The Gordie Brown Showroom at the Golden Nugget. 129 Fremont Street. 866-946-5336.

Watching Downtown Las Vegas' pre-eminent entertainment act morph through his repertoire of five-dozen celebrity personas in 80 minutes makes you break a sweat in your seat. The comic is so talented and so fast he practically

Gordie Brown

Julian LeBallister/Golden Nugget Hotel & Casino

leaves Robin Williams at the starting gate as he sprints through the spirit of each character he channels, giving them voice and even original jokes they would have invented and delivered in their own style.

It's difficult enough to catch the character of another person, but Brown sings in their voice, puckers in their facial contortions, leans into their stance, and moves into their head – in staccato fashion, one character to the next, barely pausing to be Gordie in-between. The audience is left breathless trying to keep up with the talent on stage, while buying into his characters, one after another, as if they were really there.

The Montreal native has been moving around Las Vegas since 1987, studying and admiring the talents of comedy impersonation greats as Rich Little and Danny Gans before getting his big break with a long-running show at the Venetian and finally landing a

GREAT IMPOSTERS

permanent gig at the Golden Nugget recently.

Dressed in a casual jeans and shirt outfit Brown might start with a Neil Diamond medley backed by a seven-piece band, and seasoned with a battery of pithy jokes to get the audience warmed up. From there he is off and running: Ted Koppel, Elton John, Mike Tyson and Garth Brooks… then you'll have a moment with Henry Fonda and Katherine Hepburn in the movie "On Golden Pond." Suddenly, it's a witty Randy Travis and even funnier Willie Nelson and Julio Iglesias, topped with a lightening fast impression of Dustin Hoffman in "Rain Man." In the next ten minutes you'll be looking at Ozzy Osbourne, Ray Charles, Stevie Wonder, a drunken Billy Joel and a sensational Louis Armstrong.

The extensive list of spirit visitors ensures everyone gets a moment with a favorite star along with a laugh, and sometimes a tear, courtesy of Gordie Brown, Tuesday to Saturday at 7:30 pm.

Legends In Concert

At Imperial Palace, 3535 Las Vegas Blvd. S. 702-731-3311 or 800-634-6441. www.imperialpalace.com.

Frank Sinatra still comes around to perform; Richie Valens pops in to entertain; and Elvis has not left the building in two decades. Deceased though these celebrities may be, their impersonations and those of others live on, brought together in this show.

Contemporary performers impersonate those celebs that time has lost, as well as those still with us—legends dead and alive are brought to life nightly in the Imperial Palace's celebrity tribute show, Legends In Concert, which celebrated its 22nd anniversary in May 2005.

Considered the granddaddy of the live-star impersonation shows, Legends in Concert is not only the original show of this type, but it's far and away the biggest.

The show changes every three months. The list of nearly 100 legends portrayed over the years includes Marilyn Monroe, Buddy Holly, Madonna, Jerry Lee Lewis, The Beatles, Dean Martin and Jennifer Lopez.

The Rat Pack is Back

At Plaza Hotel & Casino, 1 Main Street. 702-386-2444 or 800-634-6575. www.plazahotelcasino.com.

This two-hour tribute to the Rat Pack (Frank Sinatra, Sammy Davis Jr., Dean Martin, Joey Bishop and Peter Lawford), with a cameo by Marilyn Monroe, starts off with a voice-over introduction by Buddy Hackett. The show then brings on Hackett's real-life son, Sandy, in the role of Joey Bishop to start the roll of gags, jokes, songs and continuous sipping in this recreation of the Copa Room show at the erstwhile Sands Hotel. They've modernized the show (the racial barbs at Davis have softened) and they try to give an even hand to the different players, each of whom performs key musical numbers and acts that reflect his career. Of course, there's still the infamous drink cart, the constant kidding, and magical chemistry similar to that shared by the real Rat Pack.

The show comes with dinner in true Old Vegas fashion.

George Wallace

Crazy World Inc.

Formerly at the Greek Isles, show's new home at the Plaza (a property that seems lodged in the 1970s) is the perfect place for this spoofing group to call home for now.

Wayne Brady

In the CHI Room at Planet Hollywood. 3667 Las Vegas Blvd., S. 702-785-9005 or 866-919-7472. www.planethollywoodresort.com

From the famous 1990s show, *Whose Line is it Anyway* with Drew Carey, to the fabulous one-man headlining show at the Venetian, Wayne Brady has had a charmed career. The multi-talented stage force has all the polish of Ben Vereen but takes his show to unpredictable places each night, ad-libbing all the way. He had a lot of practice at this genre during his television tenure. The show centered on four performers who would create skits, scenes and songs on the spot according to topics raised by the audience. Brady has since moved through his own televised talk shows to

Comedy Central's *Chappelle's Show* to become a force among the progressive voices of comedy and satire, especially in the leagues of Spike Lee, Wanda Sykes, DL Hughley, and Paul Mooney. Talent and versatility prevent Brady from fitting squarely into any hole. At the Venetian's Showroom Brady keeps the entertainment piqued with spontaneous skits and performances, plus songs from his own line-up of hits.

George Wallace

At Flamingo, 3555 Las Vegas Blvd. S. 702-733-3333 or 888-902-9929. www.georgewallace.net.

Part gospel revival, part Red Foxx redux, George Wallace keeps audiences singing and laughing and tapping through a very entertaining 90 minutes in a show that is different every night. The talk and comedy part of the show pokes fun at everyday situations, lands a litany of "Yo Mama" jokes but stays entertaining all the while.

65

ANIMAL ACTS

Some of the best acts in Vegas have fins. Others have fur. Either way, they love the bright lights and know how to claw—or swim—their way to the top. The best part is, they work for food!

Shark Reef

Las Vegas News Bureau

Shark Reef★★

At Mandalay Bay, 3950 Las Vegas Blvd. S. 702-632-7777 or 877-632-7400. www.sharkreef.com. Open year-round daily 10am–11pm. $16.95 adults, $10.95 children (ages 5-12; ages 4 & under free).

Just when you thought it was safe to go back into the casino, along comes an adventure that grips you in the "Jaws" of excitement. Shark Reef at Mandalay Bay is not your typical aquarium.
This total sensory experience takes you on a journey through an ancient temple that has been slowly claimed by the sea. You wind up on the deck of a sunken treasure ship in shark-infested waters. Developed in consultation with the Vancouver Aquarium Marine Science Center in Vancouver, Canada—one of the world's most respected marine facilities—the 90,560-square-foot Shark Reef is home to a diverse cross-section of magnificent aquatic creatures, including different species of sharks, exotic fish, stingrays, reptiles and turtles.
Featuring more than 2,000 specimens, the reef holds nearly 1.6 million gallons of seawater among its 14 exhibits.

Treasure Bay – Meet four different species of sharks—tiger, sandbar, lemon and nurse—along with majestic green sea turtles and a variety of fish.
Crocodile Habitat – Encounter rare golden crocodiles, a hybrid between saltwater and Siamese crocs.
Lizard Lounge – Get up close to 9-foot-long monitor lizards—if you dare.
Touch Pool – Discover what shark skin really feels like, examine the shell of a horseshoe crab, and learn how sea stars swim along the ocean floor.

MUST SEE

The Lion Habitat★

At MGM Grand, 3799 Las Vegas Blvd. S. 877-880-0880. www.mgmgrand.com. Open year-round daily 11am–10pm. Free.

MGM Grand guarantees visitors the lion's share of excitement at the hotel's renowned Lion Habitat. Located inside the casino next to Studio 54, the tri-story structure showcases a variety of African lions and cubs, including Goldie, Metro and Baby Lion (a direct descendant of MGM Studio's signature marquee lion, Metro).

Besides adding an adventurous element to the hotel, the lion habitat truly educates guests about these magnificent creatures. You'll see lions up, down and all around as they romp throughout the $9 million, 5,345-square-foot structure, which is enclosed by glass and encased by skylights. The habitat boasts 35-foot-high walls, allowing visitors the opportunity to watch the lions' every move; and move they do. The lions can prowl above and below you at any time, via a see-through walkway tunnel running

To Ride With Lions

Evans transports lions from his property, which is 12 miles from the **MGM Grand**, to the hotel two to three times a day. Accustomed to humans, and comfortable in front of a camera, the felines are at home being up-close and personal with their human counterparts. There are between one and five animals in the habitat at any given period; no group stays in the structure for more than six hours at a time.

through the habitat. Veteran animal trainer Keith Evans owns, oversees and trains the animals. He also helped design the habitat. Adorned with trees and foliage, and featuring four waterfalls, multiple overhangs and a pond, the habitat is designed to be a splendid and humane showcase for the majestic creatures.

Admission is free but you can take your photo with lions nearby and shop at the habitat gift store where a portion of the purchase will go to lion preservation.

Lion Habitat at the MGM Grand

Darrin Bush/Las Vegas News Bureau

ANIMAL ACTS

The Secret Garden of Siegfried & Roy★

At The Mirage, 3400 Las Vegas Blvd. S. 702-791-7111 or 800-627-6667. www.miragehabitat.com. Open Mon–Fri 11am–5:30pm, Sat–Sun 10am–5:30pm. $15 adults, $10 children (ages 4-12).

It's probably the best-kept secret in town. Lush manicured grass, graceful palm trees, bright flowers, and crystal-clear waterfalls and pools abound within the borders of this paradisical park. In the background, the calls of exotic birds and jungle drums play over loudspeakers.

You may hear a few roars now and then, but that's just the garden's feline residents itching to share with the public the great news about this 15-acre wildlife refuge. That is, what the founders of the place, world-renowned illusionists Siegfried & Roy, for years Las Vegas' best-known, tiger-loving headliners, most cherish about it: that some of the world's rarest animals live here in harmony with one another and with humans. More than 70 animals reside within the sanctuary, including white tigers, white lions, Bengal tigers, panthers and snow leopards. With only chain-link fences separating animal from human, the $13-million jungle habitat showcases these beasts in their natural environment with ample amounts of space for play and exercise.

Behind the garden, unseen by the public, there's an indoor-outdoor compound the size of two football fields that includes catwalks 100 feet in length for exercise purposes and an air-conditioned structure housing an animal hospital, clinic and nursery.

It's a quiet place of wonder here, a Secret Garden, indeed.

White Tigers

White with black stripes, pink paws and pale blue eyes, white tigers are are not albinos. They are a genetic variation that lacks dark pigmentation. White tigers born in the wild rarely survive because they lack the natural camouflage that hides them from their enemies.

Secret Garden of Siegfried & Roy

Las Vegas News Bureau

MUST SEE

A Fish Story

More than 500 individual fish representing more than 100 species inhabit the **Atlantis Aquarium**. The fish range in size from two inches to a 4-foot-long nurse shark, the largest in the aquarium.

The Atlantis Aquarium

At The 🏛 Forum Shops at Caesar's Palace, 3570 Las Vegas Blvd. S. 702-893-3807. http://bit.ly/AtlantisAqu. Tours available daily at 1:15pm & 5:15pm.

"Don't bite the hand that feeds you" is the golden rule at the Atlantis Aquarium, where you can watch divers feed the fish twice daily. The backdrop to the **Lost City of Atlantis** animatronic statue show, this 50,000-gallon marine aquarium contains a variety of brightly colored tropical fish. The standout notables among the species, however, are the sharks and stingrays. Make sure you drop by at 3:15pm or 7:15pm, when you can witness the feeding frenzy as divers enter the tank. The aquarium offers a below-the-scenes tour of the facilities during the week *(dive shows & tours are free of charge).*

The Dolphin Habitat

At The Mirage, 3400 Las Vegas Blvd. S. 702-791-7111 or 800-627-6667. www.themirage.com. Open Mon–Fri 11am–5:30pm, weekends 10am–5:30pm. $15 adults, $10 children (ages 4-12). Admission includes Secret Garden of Siegfried & Roy.

Adjoining Siegfried and Roy's tropical Secret Garden, behind the Mirage, the Dolphin Habitat makes a huge splash with visitors year after year. Its purpose is to provide a sanctuary for Atlantic bottlenose dolphins and to educate the public about marine mammals and their environment.

It's also a research and breeding facility. The habitat makes contributions to the current knowledge about reproduction. All the dolphins housed here have been relocated from other marine-mammal projects across the country.

Dolphin Habitat

MGM Resorts International

Wildlife Habitat

At Flamingo Las Vegas. 3555 Las Vegas Blvd. S. 702-733-3111 or 800-732-2111. www.flamingolasvegas.com. Open year-round 24 hours. Free.

The Flamingo, once the secret home of Bugsy Siegel and Virginia Hill, is now the habitat of an assortment of exotic birds, fish and turtles, which hang out around a comely rock pond and a 15-acre tropical garden near the pool. See live Chilean flamingoes and an assemblage of koi, tortoises and swans, all free for the observing. Be sure to come by at 8:30am and 3pm for feeding time.

ANIMAL ACTS

WEDDING CHAPELS

Getting hitched Vegas-style can make saying "I do" as easy as buying a burger or as elaborate as an episode of HBO's 2005 series *Rome*. With nearly 130,000 marriage licenses issued last year, someone ties the knot here every 14 minutes (that rate doubles on New Year's Eve and triples on Valentine's Day).

How can you join the fun?

All you need is proof of age (a driver's license, passport or birth certificate); a social security number (foreigners who exchange wedding vows in the US may need special documentation to guarantee the marriage is recognized in their country); parental consent; a court order (if participants are under age 16); and $55 for the license. No blood test. No waiting period. *For details, contact Clark County Marriage License Bureau (200 South Third St., 1st floor; 702-455-4416 or 702-455-4415; www.co.clark.nv.us/clerk/marriage_information.htm).* Whether you want to get married by Elvis, elope like Cleopatra or dash off your vows with your morning coffee, there are more than 50 chapels to do the job. Most Strip resorts have at least one chapel, and often two or three, with a full staff of wedding experts to help with the planning. These can be simple to elaborate ceremonies

Viva Las Vegas Wedding Chapel

Las Vegas News Bureau

Wild, Wild Weddings

Las Vegas offers no shortage of creative ways to get married. Here are a few suggestions for one-of-a-kind nuptials:

♦ Get married on a gondola with a serenading gondolier at **The Venetian**.
♦ Have a pirate swoop down to deliver your rings as you are pronounced man and wife on a tattered and tough pirates' ship at **TI**.
♦ Say "I do" 1,000 feet above The Strip at **Stratosphere Tower**.
♦ Have a Roman wedding, complete with sentries and sultry slave girls, at **Caesars Palace**.
♦ Crash your own wedding in a Pink Cadillac driven by and then officiated by Elvis at Viva **Las Vegas Wedding Chapel**.
♦ Get married with George Clooney or Brad Pitt or Jennifer Lopez at your side at **Madame Tussaud's**. Say "I do" by your favorite best man and maid of honor—there are more than 100 waxen celebrities to pick from. A $1,200 package can manage it all, from the limo rides and rose bouquets to wedding photos with the men and women of your dreams.

MUST SEE

and in some lush and floral settings near pools and falls. Other settings, such as the **Little White Chapel**, built in 1950 near downtown Las Vegas, remain a favorite for their kitschiness. It has half-a-dozen pews, an Elvis officiante on call, and a Tunnel of Vows, where for a $40 ride you can become husband and wife *(1301 Las Vegas Blvd. S.; 702-382-5943 or 800-545-8111; www.littlewhitechapel.com)*.

Viva Las Vegas Chapel

1205 Las Vegas Blvd. S.
702-384-0771 or 800-574-4450.
www.vivalasvegas.com.

Elvis is always at the ready in the Viva Las Vegas Wedding Chapel. This former motel has two traditional chapels and several smaller themed locations that can be put to use on that wedding day. These include the 1950s diner room, complete with juke box and soda fountain, the gazebo and the garden. Within any chosen venue, VLV can dress it up for a kitschy wedding party. Cookie cutter ceremonies include Elvis Blue Hawaii, Beach Party, the Egyptian Tut Hut, Rocky Horror, Liberace—just name your favorite fantasy scene. The chapel keeps yarmulkes and rings on hand and a picture perfect pink 1950s Caddie convertible to rush couples—or fools—into their special ceremony.

Graceland Chapel

619 Las Vegas Blvd. S.
702-382-0091 or 800-824-5732.
www.gracelandchapel.com.

Naturally, Elvis is the key to this chapel, which claims to be the one that started it all—Elvis Nuptials,

that is. Traditional weddings can also happen in this chapel that looks more like a church in the meadows than something from Graceland. Celebs to tie the knot here include Bon Jovi, Billy Ray Cyrus and Aaron Neville.

Little Church of the West

4617 Las Vegas Blvd. S.
702-739-7971 or 800-821-2452.
www.littlechurchlv.com.

Dating back to 1942, this church has seen it all in Las Vegas. The second oldest church in town (after Wee Kirk o' the Heather) still retains its original charms in all the original settings. It's a simple wooden abode with a steeple in an arbored yard, but it can hold 50 inside, although there's ne'er an Elvis in sight.

Famed "I dos" include Zsa Zsa Gabor and George Sanders, Judy Garland, Mickey Rooney, Dudley Moore, Richard Gere and Cindy Crawford. Britney Spears even married here in 2004 for all of 55 hours, before having the "joke" marriage annulled.

A Special Memory Wedding Chapel

800 S. Fourth St.
702-384-2211 or 800-962-7798.
www.aspecialmemory.com.

If you really can't wait, this is the chapel for you. No fuss, no muss, you can even stay in your car. The chapel performs "drive-thru" ceremonies for $25 (plus $40 for the minister). It also offers sit-down services with interior spaces for up to 110 guests, and an outdoor gazebo for smaller affairs.

VEGAS FOR FREE

Who says you can't get something for nothing? Some of the best things in life are free in Las Vegas. That includes the pleasures derived from the city's many physical attractions—at least those of the inanimate variety....

Bellagio Fountains

Las Vegas News Bureau

Bellagio Fountains★★

At Bellagio, 3600 Las Vegas Blvd. S.
702-693-7111 or 888-987-6667.
www.bellagioresort.com.

The Fountains of Bellagio are undoubtedly the big shot of The Strip. Twice an hour (or, at night, every 15 minutes) the 1,100 fountains shoot as high as 240 feet into the air, choreographed to music including everything from the classic arias of Luciano Pavarotti to show tunes, and from Liberace to the romantic stylings of Frank Sinatra. More than a thousand fountains dance in front of the hotel. At just barely under 20 million gallons and 8.5 acres, Lake Bellagio is easily the largest musical fountain system in the world. Watch it from across the street—a sidewalk table at Paris' Mon Ami Gabi speaks romance.

Bellagio Conservatory and Botanical Gardens★

Just beyond the lobby at Bellagio, you'll find the lovely conservatory garden with its 50-foot-high glass ceiling. The ceiling framework and beams are sculpted in floral patterns from oxidized copper, called verde. With the change of each season, the garden puts on a different face, with new trees and flowers. It also puts on spectacular displays for Thanksgiving, Christmas and the Chinese New Year.

Las Vegas News Bureau

MUST SEE

Fremont Street Experience★★

425 Fremont St. 702-678-5777. www.vegasexperience.com.

If you're traveling downtown from The Strip, it may feel like Las Vegas has disappeared somewhere between St. Louis Avenue and Fremont Street. Don't give up, just keep on going and you'll definitely see the light. Or lights, in this case—more than two million light bulbs to be exact, down on Fremont Street. Since it opened in December 1995, the Fremont Street Experience has turned up the wattage in downtown Las Vegas every night with a spectacular computer-generated sound-and-light show. The Experience is a modern technological and engineering marvel, clearly one of a kind. Suspended 90 feet over downtown, a four-acre barrel-arched canopy jolts to life several times nightly above a four-block section of Fremont Street *(between Main & 4th Sts.)*. Holding it aloft are 16 columns, each weighing 26,000 pounds and each capable of bearing 400,000 pounds. The illuminated extravaganza of flashing, rolling images is generated by more than two million fiber-optic lights and synchronized to music from a 540,000-watt sound system. Created by a consortium of 11 casinos, the attraction has transformed downtown's five-block principal thoroughfare into a mix of urban theater and a variety of dining, entertainment and shopping venues. Under its high dome, the canopy creates a pedestrian mall closed to traffic and encompassing several of Las Vegas' most popular downtown casinos, including the Golden Nugget.

"Watts" up on Fremont Street?

- ◆ 180 computer-programmed, high-intensity strobe lights.
- ◆ 64 variable-color lighting fixtures that can produce 300 colors.
- ◆ 8 robotic mirrors per block that can be individually programmed to pan and tilt to reflect light.

Mirage Volcano★★

At The Mirage, 3400 Las Vegas Blvd. S. 702-791-7111 or 800-627-6667. www.themirage.com.

The Mirage volcano, no longer a mere 54-foot leap of middling flames, is now an immersive

Fremont Street Experience Show

Brian Jones/Las Vegas News Bureau

Mirage Volcano

Las Vegas News Bureau

explosion of fire, water and sound that will simply take your breath away—possibly steaming it first. With a recent $25-million magma lift (that debuted in December 2008), the iconic Strip volcano more than doubled its incendiary reach to 120 feet and also doubled its running time to 4.5 minutes. New 'FireShooters' designed by WET (think Bellagio fountains, Bellagio Conservatory, the fountains for 1998 Lisboa Expo, the cauldron for the 2002 Olympic Winter Games), plus new water design and steam elements, a rock design for the volcano and an expanded meandering tropical lagoon makes for a traffic stopper and crowd pleaser that only Las Vegas could execute.

The icing on this cake (shall we say plume of this caldera?) is the music. Beyond the mesmerizing conflagration is a percussive build to a riveting crescendo composed by legendary Grateful Dead drummer Micky Hart and Indian Tabla sensation Zakir Hussain. The seven-movement oeuvre contains indigenous music and soundscapes and some one-of-a-kind instruments heard nowhere else. Timed to complement the performances of the Sirens of TI, crowds packing along this mid-Strip stretch will not be disappointed.

The Sirens of TI

At Treasure Island, 3300 Las Vegas Blvd. S. 702-894-7111 or 800-944-7444. www.treasure islandlasvegas.com.

Since its inception, *The Pirate Battle of Buccaneer Bay at Treasure Island* was always what the name implied—a 12-minute fight to the finish between a British frigate, the HMS *Britannia*, and a pirate ship, the *Hispaniola*.

In tandem with the hotel's tenth anniversary in 2003, a new show called *The Sirens of TI* was unveiled. A sensual, modern interpretation of the Pirate Battle, male pirates are now joined by female sirens, who are part muse, part seductress and part pirate. Directed and choreographed by Kenny Ortega (of *Dirty Dancing* fame), the show is a modern pop musical with singing, dancing, feats of amazing strength, pyrotechnics and sound. Ortega claims that ancient Greece's legendary sirens were his inspiration for the storyline.

Sirens of TI

Las Vegas News Bureau

MUST SEE

⚓ Circus Circus Big Top

At Circus Circus Hotel & Casino, 2880 Las Vegas Blvd. S. 702-734-0410 or 877-634-3450. www.circuscircus.com.

When this property opened in 1968 it was a first for Vegas—a hotel that provided something for kids to do while their parents gambled. It's still a unique destination along The Strip. A literal three-ring circus, which bills itself as the world's largest permanent circus, surrounds the casino with real circus acts performed day and night. Even hardcore slot-pullers take a break to watch the trapeze artists swing from the heights above them. Dazzling aerialists, trapeze artists, magicians, contortionists and clowns shows are just a few of the myriad performers that give shows free-of-charge twice an hour daily, from 11am to midnight.
Catch the spectacular juggling feats of renowned performers who hail from Moscow and Moldavian circus troupe as well as the acrobatic, trapeze and aerialists antics of The Sandou Troupe. The acts change, so you will see different feats if you come back later.

Festival Fountain Show

At The ⚓ Forum Shops at Caesars Palace, 3570 Las Vegas Blvd. S. 702-893-4800. www.harrahs.com.

You can't help but be amazed at the new level of animatronics and laser lighting that the Festival of Fountains boasts. The party starts at 10am, when Bacchus, god of

Festival Fountain Show

Caesars Entertainment

wine, wakes up and decides to throw a party for himself. He enlists the powers of Apollo, god of music; Venus, goddess of love; and Plutus, god of wealth. As the festivities begin, the statues talk and move, enhanced by animatronics and laser special effects.
The entire show is controlled by computer. Each statue's voice is a scripted recording that runs on a cue list that "talks" to the computer. There are over 700 cues for one entire show, which lasts eight minutes—the memory of it lasts much longer. A second dramatic fountain show of exploding fire and ice runs hourly in the middle wing of the complex.

Masquerade Show in the Sky

At Rio, 3700 W. Flamingo Rd. 702-777-7777 or 800-752-9746. www.riolasvegas.com.

A $25-million interactive entertainment experience, Masquerade Show in the Sky reflects the spirit of Brazil's

Lake of Dreams

When **Wynn Las Vegas** opened in 2005 it was not without the casino mogul's trademark "wow" attraction. But this one was for the inside crowds only. Lasers, animated projections, a medley of sound and light – and a storyline, are all choreographed here on a stunning canvas of a foggy shrouded lake, waterfalls and the 140-foot. mountain that separates Wynn from the rest of Las Vegas. Two types of shows spring to action at the top and bottom of the hour when the sun goes down. Some 4,000 lights project onto the falls and lake, set to music on the bottom of the hour. At the top of the hour is the primary attraction, which includes a large movie screen element synched to the imagery and music that changes from show to show. See it all for a serene sip at the e Parasol Lounges.

Carnivale. The show consists of five complete parades—Village Street Party, South of the Border, Carnivale, Venice Masquerade and New Orleans Mardi Gras, which alternate throughout the day. Each 12-minute show has different music, costumes and performances by a 26-member cast.

Five performer-filled floats, each boasting its own individually themed music and sound system, move on a 950-foot track 13 feet above the casino floor of Masquerade Village. For a small fee, you can dress in costume and climb aboard one of the floats to cavort with the entertainers. There is a catch—and hopefully it's yours as the entertainers throw out bright strands of beads from the floats to the crowds below.

Neon Museum

East end of Fremont Street Experience, downtown. 702-387-6366. www.neonmuseum.org. Open year-round 24 hours.

The Neon Museum was erected in 1996 out of the ashes of the Neon Boneyard, where all good electric signs must someday go to die. A living, outdoor exhibition area on the far side of the Fremont Street Experience, the museum takes visitors on a sentimental walking journey, past the famed Hacienda Hotel's horseman and the golden bulbs of Aladdin's Lamp (from the original Aladdin Hotel structure) to the c.1961 Flame Restaurant sign, pulsing on the roof of the restaurant once located on Desert Inn Road.

You'll also see the Chief Hotel Court sign from the 1940s, when the hotel was located on that street. The hotel continues along the pedestrian corridor of Fremont Street and is dotted with odd souvenir and notion shops and the more recent Neonopolis mall and theater complex.

🏛 Town Square

6605 Las Vegas Blvd. S.
www.townsquarelasvegas.com

Land is eminently available and relatively inexpensive as you inch south of The Strip toward LA. The newest shopping center to emerge in this developer's heaven is the eighth such mega mall to grace Las Vegas Blvd. between Spring Mountain and Warm Springs roads. The sprawling 1.5-million-square-foot development claims to be a "lifestyle center," and indeed this small town of big chain stores offers a slice of life on Main Street Barcelona, Main Street Milan, Main Street Casablanca and Main Street San Diego. The developers have tried to side-step the uniformity of your usual model town by injecting, Botox style, some 70 different "façade types," into the architecture. Vegas' familiar promenades and skyscrapers give way here to small tree-lined streets—with parking meters ($1/hr)—and two-story buildings. Over 150 shops, more than a dozen restaurants and several entertainment venues keep it all interesting. The lengthy list of retailers includes The Strip's second Apple Store. Diners will find Tommy Bahamas Tropical Café intriguing; shop for shirts then sip Mai Tais on the patio overlooking the park. Yes, there is a park, just a like a real town, or a Vegas town at least. This 9,000-square-foot patch is the centerpiece of the project with a hedge maze, a 25-foot high tree house, pop-up fountains, a Tom Sawyer house, a mini replica of the center, storytelling stages and plenty of park benches for tired mall rats.

🔥 Fremont Street East

5th to 7th Streets along Fremont St.

Downtown Vegas is experiencing a retro renaissance. Once you've had your ten minutes of bedazzlement watching the corridor canopy of Fremont Street's "Vivavision," head to the Downtown territory known as Fremont Street East, along Fremont. This is the city's arthouse entertainment district where bohemian denizens flock to such hot spots as The Beauty Bar *(517 Fremont St., 702-598-1965, www.beautybar.com)*, well-known to Angelenos for its Hollywood flagship. It swells with vintage interiors: beauty stations for pedicures and Pernod, a genre-embracing soundtrack and a funky back door patio. Next door is the Griffin *(511 Fremont St., 702-382-0577)*, a dark, somewhat goth, drinking establishment with a central fireplace and castle-like motifs. The promenade brings plenty of vintage Vegas neon with it and extends an area of Fremont Street that has seen a proliferation of upmarket and casual scene bars and restaurants in recent years. Watch for the old, bulb-busting Silver Slipper shoe—all aglow again.

Beyond Buskers

You don't have to wander the streets of Venice or Las Ramblas of Barcelona to see human statues masking as fine art. The **Canal Shoppes** at the Venetian has taken a tip from its European counterparts and put their own street artists to work creating a mall gallery of human statuary and lively street performance. They call it "Streetmosphere" here, but unlike the ambient cobbled sidewalks of the old country, no hats are passed. You need not shell out those quarters and dollars to hear a trio of tenors dressed in Renaissance garb breaking into a familiar aria or two. Stay around as long as you like. There is even a St. Mark's Square where you can have your latte and gelato and not have to shoo away the bird life while watching a steady stream of artists entertain.

MUSEUMS

It has often been said that good things come in small packages. So it is with Nevada's museums and art galleries. Although Las Vegas is hardly known for its museums, the city has come a long way in equipping itself with unique museum offerings.

The Atomic Testing Museum★★

755 E. Flamingo Rd. 702-794-5161. www.atomictestingmuseum.org. Open year-round Mon–Sat 9am–5pm, Sun 1pm–5pm. Closed Jan 1, Thanksgiving Day & Dec 25. $12.

Las Vegas may be ground zero for the largest hotels on the planet, but did you know it was also ground zero for friendly nukes from 1951 to 1992? This well-curated museum, designed with assistance from the Smithsonian Institution, recounts the history of atomic testing in the US—the good, the bad, and the ugly—through newsreel videos, painstakingly detailed environmental recreations, and brilliantly interpreted explanations. You'll even get to experience a simulated atomic explosion from the confines of a sealed underground room (not for the claustrophobic). What's so impressive about the 8,000-square-

foot space tucked into the Desert Research Institute is not so much what you see, but the resources that are available at every turn. From the library to the gift shop, you'll find former test-site employees and engineers eager to talk about the reality of life on that off-limits, 1,400-square-mile, pock-marked, radioactive preserve located 65 miles northwest of Las Vegas, and debunk the myths that continue to swirl around the secrecy of operations there.

Bellagio Gallery of Fine Art★★

3600 Las Vegas Blvd. S. 702-693-7919. www.bellagio.com. Open year-round Mon–Fri 10am–6pm (Fri, Sat until 9pm). $15 (includes audio tour). Reservations strongly advised.

With the creation of the Bellagio Gallery of Fine Art, the first gallery on The Strip, it became

Atomic Testing Museum

Brian Jones/Atomic Testing Museum/Las Vegas News Bureau

Bellagio Gallery of Fine Art

clear that art in Las Vegas was no longer being given the brush-off. The facility is a noncommercial venue dedicated to presenting high-quality art exhibitions from major national and international museums. It generally brings in two exhibitions a year from the world's greatest art collections, each on display for a period of six months. Past exhibits have included the works of Andy Warhol, Alexander Calder and Peter Carl Fabergé. The gallery offers a self-guided audio tour, so you can stop before any painting and listen to the details about that particular work.

The Auto Collections★

At Imperial Palace, 3535 Las Vegas Blvd. S. 702-794-3174. www.autocollections.com. Open year-round daily 9:30am–9:30pm. Free passes available online.

You've got wheels—lots of them—at the Imperial Palace Auto Collection. Regarded as one of the finest collections of its kind in the world, the exhibit showcases more than 750 antique, classic and special-interest vehicles spanning

nearly 200 years of automotive history. Of these, more than 200 are on display—and for sale—at any one time in a gallery-like setting on the fifth floor of the Imperial Palace's parking structure. The constantly rotating collection features vehicles once owned by famous people (James Cagney, Elvis Presley, Al Capone, Benito Mussolini). The collection also displays the rarest and some of the most exclusive and historically significant cars ever produced, including the world's largest collection of Model J Duesenbergs.

Holy Car!

The **1934 Ford V8 cara** of Bonnie and Clyde is on display at Terrible's Primm Valley Resort & Casino just outside Las Vegas. The ghostly relic bears the scars of some 167 bullets fired in an ambush shoot-out with the law outside a remote Louisiana parish after the couple had managed to kill more than two dozen others. The car was sold to Primm for $250,000 and remains a popular and free attraction.

MUSEUMS

Madame Tussauds Las Vegas★

At The Venetian, 3377 Las Vegas Blvd. S. 702-862-7800. www.madametussauds.com/lasvegas. Open year-round daily 10am–10pm (last tickets sold 10pm). $25.

What do Tom Jones, Wayne Newton, Engelbert Humperdinck, Mick Jagger, Oprah Winfrey, George Clooney, Brad Pitt and more than 100 other celebrities have in common? They all have what it takes to get their likeness in Madame Tussauds Las Vegas at the Venetian. When it comes to the making of a star, Madame Tussauds has broken the mold. In this case, spinning off 105 to 110 masterfully crafted molds. Here you'll find realistic wax figures of some of the world's most popular film, television, music and sports celebrities, as well as legendary Las Vegas icons. They're all showcased at the Venetian's special two-story Las Vegas site. At Madame Tussauds, you can have your picture taken with your favorite stars—even marry

them, sort of—just don't expect them to be animated about it. As unbelievably lifelike as they look, the only thing real about the figures is the clothing (most of the celebrities donated the garb that is presented). New figures include Hugh Hefner, Cameron Diaz and the Blue Man Group.

A Las Vegas exclusive is Evel Knievel in his prime in the mid 1970s in his red, white and blue jumper and trademark cane. You can even sit on an authentic replica of one of his bikes—a 1972 Harley Davidson XR750, put on a themed Evel cape, and have your photo taken with the bike and Evel's life-like figure. A looping video of the dare-devil's feats—and crashes—plays in the background. Putt with Tiger, size up with Shaq. They're all here.

Nevada State Museum and Historical Society★

700 Twin Lakes Dr. 702-486-5205. www.nevadaculture.org. Open year-round daily 9am–5pm. Closed Jan 1, Thanksgiving Day & Dec 25. $4.

This museum's story is Nevada's history, and this nationally accredited institution tells it with

President Barrack Obama, Madame Tussaud's

Glenn Pinkerton/Las Vegas News Bureau

The Las Vegas Mob Experience

Denise Truscello/The Las Vegas Mob Experience

authority—from the wanderings of a 225-million-year-old ichthyosaur in the Mojave Desert to tourists prowling modern-day Las Vegas. Located in a pretty park with a duck pond, not far from downtown Las Vegas, the Nevada State Museum's permanent exhibits focus on the natural and anthropological history of the region. Don't miss the recorded story of "Bugsy" Siegel's Flamingo Hotel, complete with his threats on his business partners' lives. The museum is one of several in Nevada, including a new one under construction in Springs Preserve.

The Las Vegas Mob Experience★

At t Tropicana. 3801 Las Vegas Blvd. S, 702-739-2662. www.lvme.com. Open daily 10am–10pm. $39.95; VIP passes for $59.95.

Tony, the Ant, may be buried in a cornfield somewhere south of Chicago, but the Mob is alive and well in Las Vegas and living at the Tropicana Hotel. This creative come-to-life museum is Las Vegas'

latest attraction and one that will soon see a sibling when a second museum dedicated to the Mafia opens next year in the former Las Vegas courthouse where gangland trials actually took place in the early 1960s.

The Mob Museum Trop-style is a meadering collection of rooms, each with their own storyline, personality and mission. The attraction employs actors who give assignments to visitors who "wanna get made." Each visitor is given a name – the Iceman, the Mouth, whatever and as they walk through the set, they get deeper and deeper in with the gang. Holograms and videos of Soprano

Not by Buffets Alone

Las Vegas was not built by buffets alone. It was money from "**back east**," that backed Bugsy's bid to put a carpet joint in the middle of nowhere - now the Flamingo at center Strip. Many of the families of the Men who Built Vegas still live in town and contributed to this museum. In fact, many say, the Mob never really left.

It (was) the Water

Las Vegas literally means **"the meadows,"** and the green carpets that once defined this desert were fed by a robust system of artesian springs. Those springs are what brought the railroad to this point in 1905 and launched what is now Las Vegas. The springs flowed for at least 5,000 years until they finally dried up in 1962.

characters help with the guidance, but in the end, you either get made or you get whacked.

And it's not always your choice. In between, through a scrupulously collected, interpreted and staged wealth of artifacts you may find more than you ever wanted to know about the Mob in Vegas in this immersive experience.

Allow at least two hours.

Las Vegas Erotic Heritage Museum

3275 Industrial Rd. 702-369-6442. www.eroticheritagemuseum.org. Open daily noon-8pm. $15.

It's only fitting that Vegas should have a museum dedicated to the Erotic Arts. This warehouse collection in western backwaters of The Strip provides plenty of reasons to wander the warehouse wastelands and find this gem. The place is chock full of stuff – a veritable hoarder's garage of antique porn videos, odd spanking and stimulation contraptions, bondage contraptions from the ages, peep machines, prostitution paraphernalia, even politics – if you buy Larry Flynt's lobbying against censorship and for 1st Amendment rights as a lesson in civics. Remember to swing by the gift shop for a look at odd items where you need not be embarrassed by browsing and buying.

The Springs Preserve

333 S. Valley View Blvd. 702-822-7700. www.springspreserve.org. Open daily 10am–10pm summer, until 6pm winter. $18.95.

The Springs Preserve is a $250-million non-gaming cultural attraction located a few miles west of The Strip with 180 acres of museums, botanical gardens, galleries, trails and entertainment elements.

An uncommon blend of interactive and educational experiences for all ages are folded into the visitor

Springs Preserve

experience, which includes: an up-close look at a living bat cave, a brush with a live flash flood, a historic trail walk that passes by a Cienega (desert wetland), or an outdoor cooking demonstration in the botanical gardens. Children can climb aboard a 50-foot rattlesnake replica in the children's playground, visit the Preserve's resource library, master one of the many educational video games in the New Frontier Gallery or trade in their own artifacts at the Nature Exchange for other desired items. Families can cap their day with a live outdoor concert in the Springs Amphitheater, a light dinner in the Springs Café (operated by Wolfgang Puck) overlooking the Las Vegas Strip, and a stroll through the Canary Project photo gallery. And while browsing, visitors need not be concerned about leaving behind their dirty carbon footprints. The structures join an elite list of buildings nationwide for "Platinum" Leadership in Energy and Environmental Design (LEED) certification from the US Green Building Council (USGBC).

Las Vegas Natural History Museum

900 Las Vegas Blvd. N. 702-384-3466. www.lvnhm.org. Open year-round daily 9am–4pm. Closed Thanksgiving Day & Dec 25. $8.

Looking for ancient sharks or dinosaurs? The Las Vegas Natural History Museum's (LVNHM) multisensory exhibits are a good way to combine education and fun for all ages. Animated exhibits, robot dinosaurs (including a 35-foot-long *Tyrannosaurus rex*), live fish and more than 26 species of preserved animals—including rare African water chevrotains (a cross between a pig and a deer), as well as zebra duikers from Liberia – take you from the neon jungle to the real jungle in a flash. There are even several "hands-on" areas where animals can be petted.

Las Vegas Gambling Museum

500 S. Main St. 702-385-7424.

Las Vegas is a museum in its own right, a quirky collection of neon, glass and water in fantasy-focused, made-to-be-imploded structures all in an improbable spot out in the middle of nowhere. And it collects its collectors, residents with their own ideas of what is valuable and interesting.

All a visitor needs to do is walk along Main Street between Stratosphere and Downtown for a living museum of antiques and Vegas lore.

The best spot for this might be Main Street Antiques. The owner once operated the Las Vegas Gambling Museum inside the Tropicana Hotel and moved the entire collection to this site. Find rooms full of Las Vegas memorabilia on display in these cavernous quarters, from chips of long-gone casinos, to famous showgirl garb worn in legendary revues to vintage neon cocktail signs—and all of it is for sale. There's even an engaging historical exhibit on the mafia presence in Sin City.

Bargaining is on the table here even if the chips are under glass. The store lies on the edge of the Las Vegas Arts District of studios and galleries and antique depots.

HISTORIC SITES

There were several phases of Las Vegas' Old West history—indeed, a couple of them notable for what happened clear out of town, in places like Boulder City and Overton. From the Wild West days to the era of large-scale local public waterworks like Hoover Dam, Vegas' colorful past comes alive at these sites.

Bonnie Springs/ Old Nevada★

1 Gunfighter Lane, Blue Diamond, NV. ◗ *From The Strip, take Charleston Blvd. west for 25mi. 702-875-4191. www.bonniesprings. com. Shuttles are available from The Strip (call Star Land Tours; 702-296-4381). Open daily May– Sept 10:30am–6pm, Oct–Apr 10:30am–5pm. $20/car includes a $10 coupon for the ranchhouse restaurant.*

The Wild West comes alive at Old Nevada, an 1880s mining town recreated on 115-acre Bonnie Springs Ranch. Nestled in Red Rock Canyon, a 30-minute drive from the Las Vegas Strip, Old Nevada provides plenty of rough-and-tumble action, including gunfights in the streets. There's also a miniature train ride, a wax museum illustrating figures from

Nevada's frontier history, a lovely 19C chapel, a restaurant, and shopping for turquoise, silver and Western souvenirs. The petting zoo, which houses deer, goats, raccoons, swans, llamas, and even a long-horned steer from Texas, is the most popular attraction on the property. On weekends, stay around for the posse show, an 1830s melodrama in which even the kids can help track down a mustachioed villain in an authentically recreated saloon. Of course, there's an obligatory public hanging with an obliging stuntman who drops haplessly from the gallows and sways in the wind. The Ranch offers 🏇 **horseback riding** with walking rides into the desert scrub. A fun thing to do here is have a hot drink on a cold day around the fire pit in the restaurant. This is a no-nonsense cowboy joint and serves great burgers. *No ties allowed.*

Old Nevada

Las Vegas News Bureau

Boulder City

Las Vegas News Bureau

Boulder City★

🕩 *23mi southeast of Las Vegas via I-93/95 North or I-515 North.* **702-293-2034. www.bouldercity.com.**

This charming little dry town (no alcohol) is the only city in Nevada that doesn't allow gaming. It was built by the government as a model city, and it has thrived on small-town values that are still very much in evidence today.

Boulder City came into existence c.1929 to house the workers constructing Hoover Dam and their families. Initially, there was some contention over where the dam was to be built—at Boulder Canyon or at Black Canyon (the latter won). Because the Boulder

Canyon Project Act had been passed before the location was changed, all plans referred to the Boulder Dam project. That's why, when the Bureau of Reclamation commissioner, Dr. Elwood Mead, personally chose the townsite, he decided to call it Boulder City. From its vantage point overlooking Lake Mead, Boulder City makes a great base for enjoying all the recreational activities the lake provides.

The city sits just around the corner *(7mi west)* from Hoover Dam. While you're here, relax in the central historic hotel plaza, browse through antique shops or grab a bite at the 1950s-style Coffee Cup Café.

Boulder's Grand Dame

Boris Karloff resided there; Bette Davis vacationed there; and Howard Hughes recuperated there after his plane crashed into Lake Mead. Will Rogers called the hotel home in 1935 when he performed at the Boulder Theatre. Built in 1933 to house government and corporate project managers overseeing the building of Hoover Dam, the Dutch Colonial-style **Boulder Dam Hotel** *(1305 Arizona St., Boulder City; 702-293-3510; www.boulderdamhotel.com)* is newly restored to its former glory after an eight-year renovation. Now a B&B, the 22-room lodging was placed on the National Register of Historic Places in 1982. Find a hidden museum of the Dam and the town here in the basement.

HISTORIC SITES

Old Las Vegas Mormon State Historic Park

© John Elk III/Alamy

What's Left of the Fort?

- **Old Fort** (1855) – The adobe building closest to the creek is the only original part of the Mormons' 150-square-foot adobe fort, which featured towers and bastions on the northwest and southeast corners.
- **Ranch House** (1865) – Octavious Gass built this ranch house using part of the Old Fort's foundation.
- **Las Vegas Springs and Creek** – Running through the ranch site is a recreation of the creek that supplied water to the area. After Las Vegas was founded, the water was diverted there, and the creek dried up.

Old Las Vegas Mormon State Historic Park ★

500 E. Washington Ave. at Las Vegas Blvd. 702-486-3511. www.parks.nv.gov/olvmf.htm. Open year-round daily 8am–4:30pm. $2.

This site was where Las Vegas began—the first permanent non-native settlement in the Las Vegas Valley. An adobe fort was built along Las Vegas Creek in 1855 by William Bringhurst and 29 of his fellow Mormons, who arrived here from Utah. The outpost, equipped with a post office, served as a way station for travelers along the Spanish Trail to California. The Mormons tried farming by diverting water from the creek, and even briefly dabbled in mining and

smelting after lead was discovered in the mountains nearby. But after two years, with internal conflicts and Indian raids, the Mormons abandoned the fort.

In 1865, Octavious D. Gass, a miner from El Dorado Canyon, bought the land and established a small store and blacksmith shop on-site. Gass defaulted on a note in 1881 and the ranch house was taken over by Archibald and Helen Stewart.

After Archibald was killed in a gunfight in 1884, Helen and her father continued to operate the ranch. In 1902 Helen sold the place along with the water rights to the San Pedro, Los Angeles & Salt Lake Railroad, which chugged into the valley in 1905. The fort was eventually renovated in 1929.

Spring Mountain Ranch State Park★

> *16mi west of Las Vegas via Charleston Blvd. 702-875-4141. www.parks.nv.gov/smr.htm. Open year-round daily 8am–dusk; main ranch house 10am–4pm. $5.*

This 520-acre ranch is located at 3,800 feet, at the base of the Wilson Cliffs in the Red Rock Canyon National Conservation Area. In the first half of the 19C, pack and wagon trains used this site, with its spring-fed creek and tranquil meadows, as a campsite and watering hole, as they headed west along the Spanish Trail.

James Wilson, an army sergeant based at Fort Mohave, and his partner, George Anderson, lay claim to the property in 1876 and named it Sand Stone Ranch. After surviving a long string of owners— including Howard Hughes—the ranch became a state park in 1971. The picturesque red main **ranch house** now serves as a visitor center. Visitors are encouraged to acquaint themselves with the area and then take a self-guided tour through the interior of the ranch house.

A guided tour of the historic area includes the two second-oldest buildings in the Las Vegas Valley: an early 19C blacksmith shop and a sandstone cabin. You'll also see the reservoir created in 1945 by former owner and radio personality Chet Lauck (dubbed Lake Harriet, for his wife), as well as the gravesites of the Wilson family, who originally homesteaded the property. Periodic living-history demonstrations interpret life on the frontier.

Blue Diamond

> *Junction of Hwy 159 and Hwy 160. 25 miles southwest of Las Vegas.*

Just down the road from Bonnie Springs and Spring Mountain Ranch is Blue Diamond, a quiet hamlet shaded by cottonwoods permanently lodged in the 1950s. About 300 people live there, read at the library and shop at the spot's only store. It's a true getaway's getaway. All is quiet here, but for the occasional sound of a barking dog or braying mule. Created in the 1940s for the workers of the nearby gypsum mine it's now a cool artifact of a time long gone.

Spring Mountains Ranch State Park

Las Vegas News Bureau

NATURAL SITES

Leaving Las Vegas for a day trip into its scenic environs can provide more than just a getaway from the action of the city. It can offer a quiet foray into some of the most interesting geological formations of the Old West.

Red Rock Canyon

Las Vegas News Bureau

Red Rock Canyon★★

❍ *Red Rock Canyon is 23mi west of Las Vegas via W. Charleston Blvd. (Rte. 159).* **Look for the sign on the right to Red Rock Scenic Drive. Red Rock Visitor Center is located at 1000 Scenic Dr. 702-363-1921. www.redrockcanyonlv.org. Hours vary seasonally. $5/car.**

A 40-minute drive from the Las Vegas Strip, the towering sandstone bluffs of Red Rock Canyon are magnificent to a fault— the Keystone Thrust Fault, to be exact, the most significant geologic feature of the canyon. Scientists think that some 65 million years ago, two of the earth's crustal

plates collided with such force that part of one plate was shoved up and over younger sandstone through this fracture in the earth's crust. Dazzling formations abound in this park carved from sand dunes cemented and tinted by water acting on iron oxide and calcium carbonate then amassing in magnificent swirls. With more than 30 miles of trails, the 300-square-mile **Red Rock Canyon National Conservation Area★★** preserves the northern end of these geologic events. The area's **Red Rock Visitor Center★** is the place to get all the information you need. A recorded tour recounts the area's ancient and natural history.

From the visitor center, you can drive the 13-mile Scenic Loop, open from 7am to dusk with panoramic views of spectacular rock formations. Highlights include **sandstone quarry★**, a 2.5-mile hike up **Ice-Box Canyon★**, and **Willow Spring**, with its ancient petroglyphs. Find picnic tables, maps and toilets at the trailheads.

Riding The Range

Horses can be rented through **Red Rock Riding Stables** (*702-875-4191*). Reserve a spot on the two-hour sunset trail ride through the canyons, which culminates with a campfire dinner.

MUST SEE

Self-Guided Driving Tour Highlights

Mouse's Tank★★ – The intriguing **Petroglyph Canyon Trail★★** (0.8mi) crosses a narrow canyon to Mouse's Tank. Named for a Paiute Indian who hid from the law here in 1897, this natural rock basin collects rainwater and provides a watering spot for birds, reptiles, mammals and insects.

White Domes Area★★ – From the visitor center, a 7-mile spur road leads to the White Domes, a landscape of mulitcolored monuments and smooth, wind-carved sandstone.

Atlatl Rock★ – On the west end of the park, a steep metal stairway climbs up to Atlatl Rock, where you'll find a rare petroglyph of an atlatl, a notched stick used to throw primitive spears.

Valley of Fire State Park★★

❯ *48mi northeast of Las Vegas via I-15 North to Hwy. 169.*
Visitor center is located on Rte. 169 in Overton, NV. 702-397-2088. http://parks.nv.gov/vf.htm. Visitor center open year-round daily 8:30am–4:30pm. Nominal fees posted at entrance.

You may think you're on Mars when you first gaze upon the jagged limestone mounds of fiery scarlet, vermillion and mauve that rise out of the stark Mojave Desert. The 56,000-acre park, dedicated in 1935 as Nevada's first state park, takes its name from its distinctive coloration. The red sandstone formations that make up this surreal scene were formed from great sand dunes during the Jurassic Period. Complex uplifting and faulting in the region, followed by 100 million years of erosion, have carved this 6-mile-long and 4-mile-wide crimson-hued valley from the desert. In the process, water and wind have shaped the land into arches, domes, spires and serrated ridges.

Valley of Fire is famous for its **petroglyphs**—ancient rock art left behind by the prehistoric Basketmaker people and the Anasazi Pueblo farmers who lived along the Muddy River between 300 BC and AD 1150.

It's wise to stop at the visitor center before exploring the area. There you can pick up maps, trail guides and books, and learn about the ecology, geology and history of the region. A drive through the valley takes about 20 minutes.

Valley of Fire State Park

Brian Jones/Las Vegas News Bureau

NATURAL SITES

Tips for Visiting

The best time to visit the preserve is in spring or autumn. **Temperatures** between mid-May and mid-September soar upwards from 100°F. The 67-mile circuit from Baker via Kelbaker Road, Kelso-Cima Road and Cima Road to I-15 is a good introduction to the park's sights.

Mojave National Preserve★

◗ *53mi south of Las Vegas via I-15, in Baker, CA; alternate entry 113mi south of Furnace Creek via I-15 to Rte. 127.*
Contact the Kelso Depot Information Center (760-252-6108). Open year-round daily 9am–5pm. www.nps.gov/moja. Park HQ at 2701 Barstow Rd., Barstow, CA. 760-252-6100.

If you're wondering just how vast and empty the desert can be, the Mojave National Preserve is the answer to your question.

An easy day trip from Las Vegas, the 1.6 million-acre preserve (which begins near Baker, California) is crisscrossed by both paved and dirt roads. The Mojave is home to nearly 300 animal species and some 700 plant species, including the nation's largest Joshua forest. The 2,500-square-mile wedge-shaped preserve encompasses a landscape of lava mesas, precipitous mountain ranges, sand dunes, limestone caverns, dry lake beds and lava tubes.

Although mines and ranches still operate in the area (watch for "no trespassing" signs), evidence of human habitation is rare. Livestock graze safely thanks to the California Desert Protection Act, and hunting is allowed, although half the preserve is designated as wilderness.

The best time to visit is March through April when carpets of wildflowers blanket the hills and canyons. But stay on trails to avoid snakes as the weather warms.

Joshua tree in Mojave National Preserve
©Andrea Hornackova/Dreamstime.com

Mojave Highlights

Hole-in-the-Wall★★ – This jumble of volcanic cliffs, one of the more bizarre geologic features of Black Canyon, is profusely pocked with clefts and cavities.
Kelso Dunes★ – The 45 acres of Kelso Dunes are among the highest in the Mojave (600 feet above the desert floor).
Mitchell Caverns★ – Six limestone caverns are concealed within the Providence Mountains, which were formed by percolating groundwater millions of years ago.

Roughing It In Style

For those who prefer civilization, the **Mt. Charleston Hotel** *(2 Kyle Canyon Rd.; 702-872-5500)* at an elevation slightly below the timberline, has a mountain lodge atmosphere with fantastic views.

The only other place for provisions is the **Mt. Charleston Lodge** *(702-872-5408)*, a popular restaurant and bar at the end of Kyle Canyon Road. If you want to escape The Strip, rent one of the log cabins, which are equipped with two-person whirlpool tubs, fireplaces and private decks.

Spring Mountains National Recreation Area★

❯ *35mi northwest of downtown Las Vegas. From The Strip, take I-15 West to Hwy. 95 North. Stay on Hwy. 95 until you get to Kyle Canyon Rd. and follow signs for Mt. Charleston. U.S. Forest Service oversees the park: 702-515-5400. www.fs.fed.us/r4/htnf/districts/smnra. Call for campground information.*

If you're pining for a beautiful alpine wilderness spot to get away from it all, **Mt. Charleston** and the surrounding Humboldt-Toiyabe National Forest is a popular destination for ⛷ **activities** like hiking, backpacking, picnicking and overnight camping.

Thick bristlecone pines (among the oldest trees on earth), clinging to the limestone cliffs 10,000 feet above the desert floor, make for an awesome backdrop.

The fifth-highest mountain in the state, at just under 12,000 feet, Mt. Charleston experiences temperatures that are usually anywhere from 20 to 40°F cooler than Las Vegas (rarely going above 80°F in the summer).

You'll notice the change in vegetation with each incremental increase in elevation. Besides the distinctive plant life, many animals inhabit the Mt. Charleston area. Among them is the Palmer chipmunk, which is found nowhere else in the world. The region is also home to bighorn sheep, elk, coyotes, bobcats, foxes and cougars.

The U.S. Forest Service maintains more than 50 miles of marked hiking trails for all abilities at Mt. Charleston. The most challenging hike is the 8.3-mile **South Loop Trail**, which climbs to the mountain's 11,918-foot summit from the head of Kyle Canyon Road. In winter there is skiing at Lee Canyon, just down the road from Mt. Charleston Lodge at the end of Hwy. 156 *(702–385-2754; www.skilasvegas.com)*.

Spring Mountains Ranch State Park near Mt. Charleston

© Ivan Cholakov/Dreamstime.com

NATURAL SITES

EXCURSIONS

You won't want to miss the boat when it comes to two of the Las Vegas area's most popular day trips, **Lake Mead** and **Hoover Dam**. If you're willing to venture a bit farther afield, within a day's drive of Las Vegas, the natural wonders of the **Grand Canyon**, the **Mojave Desert** and the **Red Rock country of Sedona**, Arizona await you.

Hoover Dam★★★

▷ 31mi southeast of Las Vegas via US-93 South. 702-294-3523. www.usbr.gov/lc/hooverdam. Open year-round daily 9am–6pm. Closed Thanksgiving Day & Dec 25. Parking $7; adult tickets $11.

One of the more impressive views in the region, this engineering wonder of the modern world supplies water for more than 25 million people. Hoover Dam was built against all odds as a WPA project during the Depression and claimed more than 100 lives in the process. Conditions were harsh, heat was horrible, wages disappeared in the nearby brothels and casinos. In 1935, the flood gates opened and the mighty

Hoover Dam, Lake Mead from the Mike O'Callaghan-Pat Tillman Memorial Bridge Walk

Glenn Pinkerton/Las Vegas News Bureau

Voices of the Damed

Some 16,000 men and women worked on the dam during its 13 years of construction. And 112 lost their lives from it, including **J.G. Tierney** who drowned while surveying and was the first fatality. His son Patrick died 13 years later to the day and was the dam's last fatality. It is said if you listen closely enough you can hear ghosts in the tunnels.

Colorado River backed up into what is now Lake Mead.

A tour of the dam is a self-guided experience that includes films, murals, exhibits, talks by knowledgeable staff in various locations, and the chance to take elevators down to the bottom of the dam, walk through a 250-foot tunnel drilled through the bedrock, and view the 650-foot Nevada wing of the power plant and its eight huge generators. Four huge 30-foot-diameter pipes transport nearly 90,000 gallons of water each second from Lake Mead to the hydroelectric generators in the powerhouse.

It takes two hours to see all there is to see at Hoover Dam during the day, but you can see a different side of the dam if you come late at night. Phosphorescent floodlights cast an eerie glow down concrete walls as the lazy Colorado flows through to Black Canyon.

MUST SEE

Grand Canyon National Park★★★

The two main access points, the South Rim and the North Rim, are 214mi apart by road. Most visitor activities in the park are located on the South Rim.

○ *To reach the South Rim, take US-93 South through Boulder City to Kingman, AZ, about 90mi; exit on Hwy. 40 East to Williams, and drive north on Hwys. 64 & 180 to Grand Canyon Village.* ○ *To get to the North Rim (open mid-May–mid-Oct; reservations advised), take I-15 North to Hwy. 9 South; go south on Hwy. 89 at Mt. Carmel junction. South Rim is 260mi east of Las Vegas in Arizona. The North Rim is 275mi east of Las Vegas. 928-638-7888. www.nps.gov/grca. Open year-round daily 24 hours. $25/car for a 7-day pass; $12 no car.*

Located in northwest Arizona, this 1,904-square-mile national park is a designated World Heritage Site. The canyon was carved over the eons by the Colorado River, and today a giant swath of the earth's geological history appears in the colorful striated layers of rock, which reach down more than a mile below the canyon's rim. At dawn and dusk, when the low-angle sun lights the vividly colored canyon walls, the 277-mile-long Grand Canyon is an awesome and humbling sight.

SOUTH RIM★★★

Grand Canyon Village – Site of the park headquarters, the main visitor center and the lion's share of hotels and restaurants and tourist facilities, this area includes the **Grand Canyon Village★** Historical District. Free shuttle bus.

East Rim Drive★★★ – The 24-mile road from Grand Canyon Village to the East Rim Entrance Station passes numerous dizzying viewpoints.

West Rim Skywalk★★ – Visitors to the western rim of the Grand Canyon can walk out beyond the precipice and see nothing but thin air all the way down to the Colorado River nearly a mile below via the Skywalk that opened in March 2007. The Skywalk is the first-ever cantilever-shaped glass walkway to suspend more than 4,000ft above the canyon's floor and extend 70 feet from the canyon's rim. *Reservations required. www.grandcanyonskywalk.com or www.destinationgrandcanyon.com.*

Visitors viewing the canyon from Lipan Point on the East Rim Drive, South Rim, Grand Canyon National Park

National Park Service/Michael Quinn

EXCURSIONS

NORTH RIM★★

Open mid-May–mid-Oct, weather permitting.

Less developed and more remote than the South Rim, the North Rim is also more spectacular, set in the deep forest of the Kaibab Plateau. **Bright Angel Point** – From the visitor center adjacent to Grand Canyon Lodge, a paved half-mile trail ends at Bright Angel Point with glorious **views★★★** of the canyon. **Cape Royal Road★** – This road extends 23 miles from Grand Canyon Lodge southeast across the Walhalla Plateau to Cape Royal. A spur route leads to Point Imperial, the highest spot on the canyon rim at 8,803 feet.

From north to south the canyon spans some 215 miles and will take about five hours to drive.

Most visitors head to the South Rim of the park as it is open all year and features the most attractions. A $25 seven-day pass to drive through the park will be required. Consider parking at Grand Canyon Village (free in most spots) and taking a hop-on-hop-off tram to such popular spots as

No Yawns Here

A five-and-a-half-hour drive from Las Vegas, the **canyon** is best visited in April, May and September, when the summer crowds have left. The 7,000-foot elevation keeps the South Rim from becoming unbearably hot in the summer; however the canyon bottom can reach temperatures of 110°F. From December to March, the upper canyon is usually snowbound. If you have more time, you can take a mule trip *(reserve several months in advance)*, or hike to the bottom of the canyon.

the historic El Tovar Hotel, Hopi House, Kolb Studio gallery and Yavapai Observation Station, all interspersed with plenty of look-outs, mini-museums, gift shops, and refreshment outlets. A National Geographic IMAX movie is worth the watch, in its location just outside the park in the village of Tusayan, South Rim. Or head to the airport there for a 30-minute helicopter ride of your life.

View from Cape Royal Road, North Rim, Grand Canyon National Park

National Park Service/Michael Quinn

MUST SEE

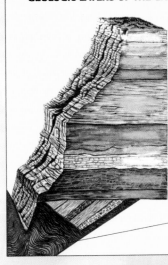

GEOLOGIC LAYERS OF THE GRAND CANYON

Kaibab Formation
Toroweap Formation
Coconino Sandstone
Hermit Shale

Supai Group

Redwall Limestone
Temple Butte Formation
Muav Limestone
Bright Angel Shale
Tapeats Sandstone

Precambrian Rocks of
the Inner Gorge

How the Grand Canyon Was Formed

In the earth's infancy, the area now defined by the Grand Canyon was covered by shallow coastal waters and active volcanoes. Over millions of years, layers of marine sediment and lava built to depths thousands of feet thick. About 1.7 billion years ago, heat and pressure from within the earth buckled the sedimentary layers into mountains 5–6 miles high, changing their composition to a metamorphic rock called **Vishnu schist**.

Molten intrusions in the mountains' core cooled and hardened into **pink granite**, then eroded. The process repeated itself: another shallow sea covering the land, more layers of sediment—12,000 foot thick now.

A new mountain range formed and eroded and the ancient Vishnu schist was laid bare. The horizontal layers above the schist, to 3,500 feet below the **modern canyon rim**, were formed over 300 million years as oceans advanced across the Southwest and then regressed.

The environment was alternately marsh and desert as dinosaurs roamed. Then the **Colorado River** began to cut the canyon about 65 million years ago, gouging through rock and carrying the debris to sea. As erosion thinned the layer of rock above the earth's core, lava spewed to the surface. In fact, there have been several periods of recent volcanic activity in the Grand Canyon area, most recently in the 11C at Sunset Crater, southeast of the park.

EXCURSIONS

It's best to visit between late autumn and early spring, as the relentless summer sun heats the valley to some of the highest temperatures on earth.
Be sure to check the gas and water in your car as well as the road conditions *(check with the visitor center)*. Always carry plenty of drinking water and know the ins and outs of survival in the desert.

Death Valley National Park★★★

❍ *120mi west of Las Vegas via I-15 South and Hwy. 160. Go through Pahrump and take State Line Rd. to Death Valley Junction; at the junction, take Hwy. 190 to the park.*
Death Valley Visitor Center is located on Hwy. 190 at Furnace Creek. 760-786-3200. www.nps. gov/deva. Open year-round daily 8am–5pm. $10-$20.

At first glance this infamous valley seems to be appropriately named, but in fact only one pioneer is known to have died trying to cross it. When you stand in this vast, silent, stark landscape, it does indeed seems inescapable.
An enormous basin (130 miles long and 5 to 25 miles wide), the valley formed progressively as a block of the earth's crust sagged and sank between parallel mountain ranges, creating an astounding difference in elevation. Altitudes range from 282 feet below sea level at Badwater to 11,049 feet at Telescope Peak. Designated as a national park under the 1994 Desert Protection Act, Death Valley is now the largest national park outside Alaska, covering more than 3.3 million acres. This is one of the hottest and driest places on earth: Annual precipitation averages less than two inches, and the highest temperature ever recorded in the US—134°F at Furnace Creek in 1913—has been exceeded only in the Sahara Desert.

Zabrieskie Point, Death Valley National Park

©PhotoDisc

MUST SEE

Furnace Creek Inn & Resort

Hwy. 190 in Death Valley National Park. 760-786-2345. 66 inn rooms; 224 ranch rooms. $340–$460, inn; $130–$215, ranch. www.furnacecreekresort.com.

There's no need to rough it in the desert when you can stay at the Furnace Creek Inn. The inn and adjacent Furnace Creek Ranch have served as a welcoming oasis for visitors since the 1930s.

You'll find everything you could ask for here—renovated air-conditioned rooms with ceiling fans, a restaurant, a spring-fed swimming pool, tennis courts, and an 18-hole golf course. The general store stocks camping supplies, but why would you want to leave this lovely place?

BEST OF DEATH VALLEY

Badwater Road★ – *Rte. 178, south of Furnace Creek.*
This 36-mile road follows Death Valley's descent to the lowest point in the Americas.

Zabriskie Point★★ – *Rte. 190, 4.5mi east of Furnace Creek.*
This renowned point commands splendid views over Golden Canyon.

Dante's View★★★ – *24mi south-east of Furnace Creek via Rte. 190 to Dante's View Rd.*
From a 5,475-foot perch atop the Amargosa Range, this stunning **view**★★★ takes in the continent's most extreme elevation change.

Stovepipe Wells Sand Dunes★★ – *6mi east of Stovepipe Wells on Rte. 190.*
The park's most accessible sand dunes pile up in billowing hills.

Scotty's Castle★ – *53mi north of Furnace Creek on Rte. 267.*
This lavish Spanish-Moorish mansion, built in 1924 as a winter retreat for Chicago millionaire Albert Johnson, is named after Johnson's flamboyant friend, Walter Scott, also known as "Death Valley Scotty."

Sedona★★

276mi southeast of Las Vegas in Arizona. Take US-93 South to I-40 East to US-89A South.
Visitor information: 928-282-7722 or www.sedonachamber.com.

This small city in northern Arizona owes its beauty and mystique to the staggering variety of striking red buttes and spires that surround it. Sedona's red rocks have been a beacon for those seeking spiritual enlightenment since the 1980s, when some of its sites (Cathedral Rock, Bell Rock, Boynton Canyon) were found to emit concentrated electromagnetic energy.

Located in the heart of Arizona's **Red Rock Country**★★★, Sedona is bounded by Oak Creek and Sycamore canyons, the Mogollon Rim and Verde Valley. The region takes its name from the rust color exposed in three mid-level strata of the Supai Group, the Hermit Formation and the Schnebly Hill Formation, all sculpted of sandstone between 270 to 300 million years ago.

Sedona's commercial area, north of the "Y" intersection of US-89A, teems with Native American craft shops and New Age boutiques. When the town gets too touristy, you're just a short drive—by

Red Rocks of Sedona

©Nick Martucci/iStockphoto.com

off-road vehicle—away from Red Rock Country. Several companies offer off-road jeep tours, but if you're driving yourself, **Schnebly Hill Road** provides the most convenient backcountry access. The 12-mile route turns from pavement to rutted dirt after the first mile, but if you press onward, you'll be rewarded by dazzling views of red rock formations and a panorama of the valley below. In the heat of summer try slipping and sliding down the natural rockslide in Oak Creek Canyon, just outside of town. Or go hunting for vortexes, areas in the earth where the magnetic forces converge to create energy pockets—or so they say. Sedona is reputed to be rife with such spots.

Lake Mead National Recreation Area★

▶ *27mi south of Las Vegas via US-93 at the junction of Lakeshore Scenic Dr. (Rte. 166). 702-293-8990. www.nps.gov/lame. Visitor center open year-round daily 8:30am–4:30pm. $5.*

Embracing two vast reservoirs on the Colorado River, this 2,350 sq mi desert preserve was created in 1936 when the natural flow of the Colorado River was blocked by Hoover Dam.
The largest manmade lake in the US, Lake Mead can hold enough water to cover the entire state of Nevada with six inches of water. More than nine million visitors each year come here to boat, fish, water

---

Rooms With A View

Montezuma Castle National Monument★ – *5mi south of Sedona in Camp Verde. Take I-17 South to Exit 289 and follow signs. 928-567-3322. www.nps.gov/ moca. Open year-round daily 8am–5pm (until 6pm in summer). $3.* Impossibly tucked into a natural limestone alcove 50 to 100 feet above the floor of Beaver Creek, Montezuma Castle was part of a 12C Sinaguan community.
Tuzigoot National Monument★ – *23mi southwest of Sedona; off Rte. 279 in Clarksville, AZ. 928-634-5564. www.nps.gov/tuzi. Open daily 8am–5pm (until 7pm in summer). Closed Dec 25. $3.* This circa 1300 Sinagua pueblo rises 120 feet above the Verde River with 86 rooms to explore.

Rollin' Round the Lake

Visit the **Alan Bible Visitor Center** *(Lakeshore Scenic Dr. at Rte. 93; 702-293-8990; www.nps. gov/archive/lame/visitorcenter)*, a few miles west of Hoover Dam to pick up information about recreational activities at the lake. Be sure to take a jaunt around the lake on the *Desert Princess*, a 100-foot triple-deck paddlewheeler that offers lunch, brunch, dinner, dancing, and even pizza cruises around the lake *(cruises depart from Lake Mead Marina near Boulder Beach; www. lakemeadcruises.com). Closed for renovations: go to: 601 Nevada Wy, Boulder City. Nevada.*

ski, swim, camp, picnic and explore. Lake Mead is the centerpiece of the Lake Mead Recreation Area, which also includes Lake Mojave to the south and the surrounding desert east and north. There are numerous sandy beaches, secluded coves and narrow canyons accessible only by water. With water temperatures averaging 78 degrees in spring,

summer and autumn, the clear lake is ideal for swimming. A fun way to explore this lake is by houseboat rental and anchoring in remote coves.

Lost City Museum of Archeology★

❍ *63mi northeast of Las Vegas. 721 S. Moapa Valley Blvd., Overton, NV. Take I-15 North to Hwy. 169 and follow Hwy. 169 through Overton. The museum is about 15mi past Overton on the right. 702-397-2193. www.comnett.net/~kolson. Open year-round daily 8:30am–4:30pm. Closed Jan 1, Thanksgiving Day & Dec 25. $3.*

The Lost City refers to the Pueblo Grande de Nevada, a series of Anasazi ruins set along the Muddy and Virgin river valleys in southern Nevada. The entire Anasazi culture, which established itself in the valley beginning about 300 BC, mysteriously disappeared from the area between AD 1150 and AD 1250. The museum was built on an Anasazi ruin and houses artifacts excavated from area Anasazi sites.

Glenn Pinkerton/Las Vegas News Bureau

Jet skiing on the Lake Mead

THRILL RIDES

Your fun factor will accelerate from 0–60 in an instant when you experience Las Vegas' thrill rides. The Gs have it in places such as Stratosphere, New York-New York, Buffalo Bill's and the Stratosphere, New York-New York and Buffalo Bill's where speed and height are the name of the game.

Sky Jump

At the Stratosphere Tower, Level 112. 2000 Las Vegas Blvd. S. 702-380-7777 or 800-998-6937. www.stratospherehotel.com. Open year-round Sun–Thu 10am–1am, Fri–Sat 10am–2am. Riders must be at least 52 inches tall. See Insanity–The Ride for prices.

Stratosphere bet the bank on building thrill rides and sanity-defying attractions that would lure in gamblers who thrive on such adrenaline shots. The Sky Jump is the latest of this series, which involves, literally leaping off the 108th floor of the Stratosphere Tower without a parachute. A zip line careens down to the sidewalk at speeds of 40mph. And these life-lines will let you down just fine for a soft enough landing that will make you want to cough up another $100 bill and do it all over again.

Sky Jump

Glenn Pinkerton/Las Vegas News Bureau

The Big Shot

If you're looking for an adrenaline rush with a bit of a safer or more controlled spin, treat yourself to the Big Shot, one of the world's highest thrill rides.

The brave hearts in this case will be one of a dozen passengers (only 12 at a time), launching from the platform to160 feet in 2.5 seconds -- up the 238-foot mast that extends like a needle from the top of the Tower, the tallest open air point in the city. You'll experience four Gs of pressure on the way up; then you'll hang suspended for a split second before hitting zero-G weightlessness on the way down. If your eyes are closed tight, you'll miss a great view of the city.

Adrenaline ATV Tours

702-289-5427 or 866-881-2887 www.adrenalineatvtours.com

Those who love to dig up the dirt can dig into the desert expanse on trails through the historic Valley of Fire through Adrenaline ATV Tours. Groups split up according to derring-do into fast, faster and fastest, allowing the most timid novice and the brashest bore to get their turf's worth along this wide open basin trail weaving around the Park that is some 24 square miles in area. Participants ride squat quad or ATV vehicles along the Logondale Trail System around the Valley of Fire that houses some of the oldest petroglyphs in the country and had been home to the Anasazi tribes and ancient Pueblo Peoples from 300 B.C. to 1150 A.D. The park is located about 50 miles (80 km) northeast of Las Vegas, by the confluence of Lake Mead National Recreation Area and the Virgin River. Riders ride through rough earth and jagged walls of brilliant sandstone formations and ancient sand dunes.

Riders are asked to tread lightly around this environment but still get their adrenaline surge along the hills, spills and blind, sharp turns they make. Tours include lunch and hotel pick-ups can be requested.

Dig This! Las Vegas Playground

3012 S. Rancho Dr. 702-222-4344 or 800-DIG-THIS. www.digthis.info.

Ever wanted to run one of those big bulldozers and just go crazy with the controls? Dig This is one of those only-in-Vegas rushes that allows you to board the cabin of a Godzilla-sized piece of earth-moving equipment and have at it in a sandbox the size of a football field. Instructions, orientation, radio, hard hat, safety vest and a pat on the back and you are ready to rock and roll as the sole operator of your own personal shoveling machine.

Never be caught short again in the cab of a bulldozer. Get the inside scoop on the in-cab controls, review communication techniques, then hit the switch as if you were made for the life of big project construction. Instructors guarantee complete comfort at the controls after the first 15 minutes. A half-day

experience includes two hours of operating time in the 15-ton excavator or the 10-ton bulldozer for $400. Age/height limits apply: 14 years old or older (under 18 requires parental consent) and 48 inches in height. Wear comfortable clothes, sturdy shoes and no smoking.

Insanity – The Ride

At the Stratosphere Tower, Level 112. 2000 Las Vegas Blvd. S. 702-380-7777. www.stratospherehotel.com. Open year-round Sun–Thu 10am–1am, Fri–Sat 10am–2am. Riders must be at least 48 inches tall. $12. Tower admission & a single ride is $19.95. Combination ticket for X Scream, Insanity and Big Shot is $27.95; an all-day unlimited thrill-ride pass at Stratosphere costs $33.95.

As the tallest structure in Las Vegas (and west of the Mississippi River) at more than 1,149 feet, the Stratosphere Tower gives thrill-seekers a hearty dose of negative Gs on its new ride. Insanity is the latest in acrophobic-challenging rides at this resort, which holds all the honors for having the highest thrill rides in the world. Named for the state of mind riders must be in to climb onto a contraption that has been described as an inverted centrifuge, Insanity is a one-of-a-kind attraction.

On this ride, ten passengers board "escape-proof" seats and are spun at 40mph over the edge of the tower, with nothing shielding them from the city more than 900 feet below. A giant arm flings folks 64 feet over the edge of the tower, then spins them at a rate that

Insanity–The Ride

Las Vegas News Bureau

induces up to three negative Gs. As the ride spins faster and faster, riders are propelled up to an angle of 70 degrees, until they are literally facing downward, looking at the city below.

⚡ Manhattan Express Roller Coaster

At New York-New York, 3790 Las Vegas Blvd. S. 702-740-6969 or 888-693-6763. www.nynyhotelcasino.com. Open year-round Sun–Thu 11am–11pm, Fri–Sat 10:30am–midnight. $14/ride; $7.00/re-ride.

Around and around and around she goes, and where she stops, you'll definitely know. Just try to smile at the end of your Manhattan Express roller coaster ride (even if you're feeling pretty green); that's when the pictures are taken. The Manhattan Express twists, loops and dives at speeds up to 60mph delivering as much as 3.7 Gs (astronauts experience 3.2 Gs on launch) as the roller coaster winds around skyscrapers and the Statue of Liberty. At times,

your whole world will literally turn upside down. This ride features the first-ever "heartline" twist-and-dive maneuver, which creates the sensation that a pilot feels when performing a barrel roll in an airplane. In this portion of the ride, the train rolls 180 degrees, suspending its riders 86 feet above the casino before diving directly under itself and into the hotel.

Manhattan Express Roller Coaster

Las Vegas News Bureau

MUST DO

🏎️ Las Vegas Motor Speedway

7000 Las Vegas Blvd. N.
702-644-4444 or 800-644-4444.
www.lvms.com.
The 1500-acre Las Vegas Motor Speedway complex includes a 1.5-mile superspeedway, 2.5-mile road course, .5-mile dirt oval and drag strip.

For adventure that truly puts pedal to the metal, Las Vegas is ground zero for auto racing. Most of the action can be found almost any day at Las Vegas Motor Speedway in North Las Vegas, a course of four different tracks used by major auto racing events including several NASCAR name-makers. The Las Vegas Metro police force trains on these tracks and so can visitors who feed on speed and want to quell their gasoline addiction. Check out Midnight Madness at the Speedway, every other Friday at the witching hour. Race your own for $15 (passengers, also $15)
The **Richard Petty Driving Experience** *(800-237-3889; www.1800bepetty.com)* straps in riders behind the wheel or in the shotgun seat of a custom-built stock car for as many as 40 laps around the 1.5-mile elliptical course at speeds of at least 150mph in the passenger seat. Packaged rates can include transfers from Strip hotels. Advanced Racing Experience packages for diehard fans can go as high as $2,599. Or, you can just ride along with a pro for $99. Indy-style racing fans hit the pavement at 145 to 180mph at the **Mario Andretti Racing School** *(877-263-7388; www.andrettiracing.com)*, which uses its own custom-built full-size single-seat cars, powered by

600-horsepower Chevy V8s with a single-speed gearbox. Participants can get their life in three short laps with the **Champ Ride**, which for $99 offers a taste of true Indy-car racing. Options available run up to $5,000 for Fantasy Day driving three different race cars with Mario Andretti graduate certificate, printed lap times, souvenir racing license and insurance.

🏎️ Zero Gravity

At McCarran Airport. 800-937-6480. www.gozerog.com.
$5,000 per person, including all taxes and fees.

Float above the neon in a reconfigured 737. The operative word here is FLOAT. Based in Las Vegas, Zero-G flights take place regularly with dates placed on the website. It could possibly be the most frightening and most thrilling ride any one will ever have and that is because it takes a plane empty of seats and galleys, covers the windows and transports around two dozen people at top speed into the upper altitudes of commercial air space. Passengers start out by lying prone on the base of the plane and float upwards as the plane dips and arcs in a series of parabolic maneuvers, ultimately mimicking the effects of weightlessness for the riders. Passengers get their fair share of 20 to 30-second floats during a three or four-hour flight. They float to piped-in music during dips and arcs through the atmosphere and take a champagne toast to their day upon landing. The experience is available out of McCarran International Airport and the costs include all the free logo gear they give you at the end. The company took physics professor and author Stephen Hawking for a test flight. The scientist, who is paralyzed from Lou Gehrig's Disease and is known for his contributions to the fields of cosmology and quantum gravity (especially in the context of black holes), was able to live out one of his dreams and float against the laws of gravity without constraint.

X Scream

At the Stratosphere Tower, Level 112. 2000 Las Vegas Blvd. S. 702-380-7777.
www.stratospherehotel.com. Open year-round Sun–Thu 10am–1am, Fri–Sat 10am–2am. Riders must be at least 48 inches tall. See Insanity–The Ride for prices (p101).

The 60 seconds that you spend dangling over Las Vegas in the seats of X-Scream will seem like an eternity. Passengers are loaded into cars that are open to the elements, with only single lap bars to keep riders in their seats. Described as a high-tech teeter-totter, the ride operates on an 86-foot track that hoists riders high into the air before diving at a 30-degree angle, wrenching both nerves and stomachs. The arm of X Scream stretches out 27 feet over the edge of the Stratosphere Tower and, after reaching speeds of 30mph, jerks to a sudden stop, taking the scream right out of frozen throats and leaving riders 900 feet above the ground to contemplate life as they knew it.

SkyDive Las Vegas

1401 Airport Road, Boulder City, 702-SKY-DIVE (759-3483) or 800-U-SKYDIVE (875-9348). www.skydivelasvegas.com. $199.

Thrill junkies who prefer to fly without a plane can book an afternoon with Skydive Las Vegas, which specializes in first-time jumpers. Participants pay per skydive but can take all the pre-flight training they want with classes running daily at 8am, 10am, noon and 2pm by appointment. Flights take off from Boulder City Airport near the Hoover Dam and, from two miles above Boulder City, with a bird's eye view of the landscape, from Lake Mead and the Colorado River, to the dam and The Strip hotels in the distance, the brave take the plunge and fall to earth at 120mph.

All jumps are tandem jumps and start at $199 including a personal keepsake video of the entire jump. Jumpers can be picked up by a van shuttle at 8am and noon from a central Strip location. The complete session lasts two to three hours and jumpers need to be in good health, under 240lbs in proportionate weight, and alert.

Flyaway Indoor Skydiving

200 Convention Center Dr. 702-731-4768 or 877-545-8093. www.flyawayindoorskydiving.com. $75, first flight; repeat is $40.

For those who want the thrill of free falling but don't want to do it hurdling to earth from a plane at 2,000 feet, Flyaway Indoor Skydiving might sound like an oxymoron but still provides

MUST DO

the 'look ma, no hands' flying experience. First, it's located just off The Strip on Convention Center Drive—no hikes along the freeway to a dirt road in the desert. Second, it's safe: The rewards for bellying up to the ticket box and paying $75 are 20 minutes of instruction, a flight suit and helmet, and a full three minutes suspended in air, no strings attached. An instructor demonstrates how to splay your body for maximum lift, and tuck and roll for maximum crash protection. Then it's off to the padded room where the propeller of a DC3 provides a wind gust of up to 120mph beneath the safety net that separates the flyers on top from a gruesome demise. Participants *(no more than ten at one time in half-hour segments 10am–10pm daily)* float about 20 feet above the net within a roaring tunnel of pure exhilaration. Do it again the same day for half price. Or, do it with friends and relatives; groups get special discounts. Kids under 18 must be accompanied by a parent and there are height and weight restrictions. Any dangers, however, are more perceived than real, in this environment.

⛷ Zipline Las Vegas

Fremont Street. 702-410-7999. fremontstreetflightline.com. $15-$20. 1512 Industrial Road, Boulder City. 702-293-6885. www.bcflightlines.com, $149.

If you feel like flying through the neon or over vast chaparral into the horizon, Las Vegas may have the thrill for you. Two flight line experiences here offer vastly different ways to fly through space. Fremont Street FlightLinez is the latest to launch, allowing visitors an affordable taste ziplining along an 800-foot course through Downtown Las Vegas. Open daily noon to midnight, closing at 2am on weekends.

Meanwhile, about 30 minutes east in Boulder City, Bootleg Canyon ⛷ **Flightlines** offers a take-no-prisoners approach for visitors who want the real thing. They launch off a mountain overlooking the desert and encounter speeds up to 50 mph as they ride into blue skies and a wide-open chaparral. The tour takes about 2.5 hours to strap in and zip down the 1.5-mile mountain course. Check times and dates for full moon tours.

Zipline Las Vegas

THRILL RIDES

WATER FUN

From pool scene (hot and sexy daylife hosted by tabloid faves are in season all summer) to beaches with real sand, Vegas is getting more wet and wild every day. Keep cool or be cool at these pool picks.

🏖 Mandalay Bay Lagoon

At Mandalay Bay,
3950 Las Vegas Blvd. S.
702-632-7777 or 877-632-7000.
www.mandalaybay.com.

Who'd ever thought you could go up a lazy river in Las Vegas? Or spend a day at the beach on The Strip? If you're a guest at Mandalay Bay, you can do both. Named in the press as one of the "sexiest" hotel pools, the 11-acre Mandalay Bay tropical water environment features a sand-and-surf beach with waves averaging 3–5 feet that

Beach Ball

You don't have to be a hotel guest to enjoy the **Mandalay Beach Summer Concert Series** that the resort presents each year. For the price of a ticket, you can lie on a towel on the sand, dip your toes in the water, and watch big-name groups (Beach Boys, Chris Isaak, Toto).

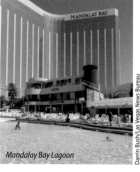

Mandalay Bay Lagoon

Darrin Bush/Las Vegas News Bureau

Gondolas at Lake Las Vegas

Situated on a private 320-acre lake, Lake Las Vegas Resort has a Mediterranean theme and a small fleet of gondolas plies the lake's placid waters, offering visitors a romantic ride. Outdoor concerts and gourmet food spice up the offering.
220 Grand Mediterra, Henderson. 17mi south of the Las Vegas Strip via US-95 South. 877-446-6365. www.gondola.com.

can be surfed by body or boogie, a lazy river, three swimming pools, and even a jogging track.
Try floating down the **Lazy River Ride** for three-quarters of a mile on a large inner tube. They don't call it "lazy" for nothing—you'll move at a relaxing snail's pace of about 2mph. Or if you really want to relax, reserve a pricey private bungalow or cabana for the day; they come equipped with snacks, drinks, a television and even a pool attendant to wait on you. Conveniently located on Mandalay Beach, the Temple Bar serves tropical drinks and a healthy selection of food. A fun "beach" casino brings gaming to the sand.

Cool Pools

In Vegas, each resort has a pool personality to match, which makes the town a museum of must-see bodies of water (not to mention the bodies in the water). It started when Tropicana built a tropical-themed pool, complete with a swim-up blackjack table. Today, Hawaiian faux lava and lush foliage are as common as C-note cabanas with special adult sections that keep the quiet in and kids out.

Hard Rock Hotel – *4455 Paradise Rd., 702-693-4440 or 800-473-7625. www.hardrockhotel.com.*
Known for its risqué pool parties—especially REHAB on Sundays, the Hard Rock sends pulsating rock music into the water for a scintillating experience of sound and sights above and below the surface.

Garden of the Gods, Caesars Palace – *3570 Las Vegas Blvd. S. 702-731-7110. www.caesars.com.*
Caesars bases its 4.5-acre Oasis of the Gods pool area on the Roman baths of Caracalla. Here you'll find eight pools stunningly adorned plaza with marble, statues, stones and columns.

Garden of the Gods pool

Las Vegas News Bureau

Bellagio Pools – *3600 Las Vegas Blvd. S. 702-693-7111. www.bellagiolasvegas.com.*
Bellagio complements its Tuscan-themed resort with six different pools, all surrounded by rose-trellised gardens and fountains.

The pricey cabanas here are tent-like structures housing a dressing area, sink, table, six lounge chairs, TV, phone, ceiling fan, mister, and a fridge stocked with fruit platters, water, ice and soft drinks.

Flamingo Las Vegas – *3555 Las Vegas Blvd. S. 702-733-3111. www.flamingolasvegas.com.*
Landscaped with waterfalls, slides, ample lounging space, lush gardens and real pink flamingos, the hotel's pool complex shares space with a wildlife habitat where penguins frolic and koi swim. A rocking adult pool area is just behind the boulders.

Four Seasons – *3960 Las Vegas Blvd. S. 702-632-5000. www.fourseasons.com/lasvegas.*
The Four Seasons' 8,000-square-foot free-form pool is a calming sunbathing heaven where attendants bring water and spray cooling mist in your face. Guests have access to the 11-acre sand and surf beach, lazy river ride, exclusive Moorea Beach Club and pools at Mandalay Bay. Other significant pool action and pool scenes can be found at MGM Grand, Encore, Cosmopolitan, Red Rock Resort, Palms, Mirage and Golden Nugget.

Bare Necessities

A new trend in Vegas' cool pool culture is **Euro-bathing**. You can find these suitless spots at the **Moorea Beach Club** at Mandalay Bay *(men pay for the privilege)*, Stratosphere, The Palms, Venetian and Caesars Palace. Costs, rules and hours vary.

WATER FUN

FOR KIDS

While much of Las Vegas doesn't kid around—nobody can pretend this is a family setting—there are several attractions and shows in the city that do focus on family fun.

Adventuredome

At Circus Circus, 2880 Las Vegas Blvd. S. 702-794-3939 or 877-224-7287. www.adventuredome.com. Open year-round Mon–Thu 11am–6pm, Fri–Sat 10am–midnight, Sun 10am–9pm. $5–$8 per ride. All-day passes, $26.95.

America's largest indoor theme park, the Adventuredome is a five-acre elevated park located behind the west tower of Circus Circus. It features the world's only indoor

Babes in Adventureland

The Adventuredome has many attractions suitable for younger children, including the traditional carousel, a roller coaster (Miner Mike) and Cliffhangers, a playspace with crawl-through tunnels, slides and more. The park offers bumper cars, carnival-style games, clown shows, arcade games and a snack bar.

double-loop, double-corkscrew roller coaster—the **Canyon Blaster**—which reaches a top speed of 55mph.

Set in a Grand Canyon motif, the Adventuredome goes out of its way to ensure that visitors get their "piece of the rock" when it comes to entertainment, packing 19 attractions under its glass dome. Since opening its doors in 1993 with four rides, the Adventuredome has welcomed more than 15 million visitors.

Other top attractions include the **Rim Runner** boat ride, which climaxes in a 60-foot water plunge,

Adventuredome

Las Vegas News Bureau

MUST DO

and **Fun House Express**, in which Chaos whirls riders in all three dimensions of motion, and the Inverter turns riders upside down. Team-laser-tag enthusiasts will want to head for **Lazer Blast**. Adventurers of all ages flock to the **Extreme Zone** to climb walls, bounce into the air on a "bungee trampoline" or try their skill at Pike's Pass, with 18 holes of miniature golf. If you'd like a high-tech motion-simulator ride, then the **IMAX Ridefilm Cineplex** is nearby, featuring Dora the Explorer in 4-D and other films that take you on a warp-speed journey through imaginary places.

Everything Coca-Cola Retail Store Las Vegas

At Showcase Mall, 3785 Las Vegas Blvd. S. 800-810-2653. Open year-round daily 10am–11pm.

If you want to keep the kids content, show them the bottle— the 100-foot-tall trademark Coca-Cola bottle in front of Monte Carlo's on The Strip. On two floors here you'll find everything you can imagine that has to do with Coke. A soda fountain on the second floor

offers ice-cream floats and other concoctions made with Coke. Here you can buy everything from a $1 souvenir to collectibles that go as high as $2,500 (for one-of-a-kind items such as memorabilia from Coca-Cola-sponsored NASCAR events).

🎮 Gameworks

At Showcase Mall, 3769 Las Vegas Blvd. S. 702-432-4263. www.gameworks.com. Open year-round Sun–Thu 10am–midnight, Fri–Sat 10am–1am.

A unique high-tech entertainment destination where you can eat, drink, party and experience state-of-the-art interactive attractions, Gameworks knows how to push the fun button for each member of the family. Here you'll find more than 200 of the newest games, many designed exclusively for Gameworks, as well as old-fashioned pinball machines. These include multisensory games based on the movies *Star Wars* and *Jurassic Park*, as well as Indy 500, Ford Racing Zone, and VR2002 Roller Coaster. There's even a five-story climbing wall.

Showcase Mall with Everything Coca-Cola Retail Store Las Vegas, Gameworks, and M&M's World Las Vegas

Las Vegas News Bureau

Gameworks also features a high-energy bar area (a good place for parents to take a break) and a full-service restaurant.

M&M's World Las Vegas

At Showcase Mall, 3785 Las Vegas Blvd. S. 702-736-7611.
www.mymms.com.
Open daily: 9 am to midnight.

Sweet smells and tastes await you at M&M's World—a four-story monument to chocolate. Each floor of this interactive shopping and retail complex offers a different layer of M&M's brand merchandise items—truly a chocolate-lover's dream.

You won't want to miss the M&M's Racing Team Shop; Colorworks, where you can sample 21 different colors of plain and peanut M&Ms; and Ethel M Chocolates, the ultimate gourmet chocolate boutique. And be sure to check out the fourth-floor ice-cream/candy shop. *I Lost My M In Vegas*, a complimentary 3D interactive movie, plays seven days a week on the third floor. Kids who "enroll" at M&M Academy may even take part in the movie.

Tournament of Kings

At Excalibur, 3850 Las Vegas Blvd. S. 702-597-7600 or 877-750-5464.
www.excalibur.com.
Shows nightly 6pm & 8:30pm.
$56.95, dinner included.

When was the last time you attended a kids' dinner theater? At the Tournament of Kings at Excalibur, it's the order of the day. A finger-licking good meal goes hand-in-hand with a genuine jousting tournament and great special effects, including dragons and fire wizards. It all makes this show a royal treat for the family. The story begins when King Arthur gathers his fellow kings of Europe for a no-holds-barred competition to honor his son.

Rival kings begin the games, gallantly riding their faithful steeds through round upon round of

Tournament of Kings

MGM Resorts International

You're Jousting!

In the **Tournament of Kings**, audience participation is an integral part of the fun. Each of the seven kings wears a different color (representing seven different countries) and the **Dragon Knight** wears black—of course. The crowd is seated in eight different sections, corresponding to a particular king and his color (or to the Dragon Knight). Sections cheer their king on, and from show to show, no one knows which one will win.

MUST DO

the medieval sport, testing their agility, strength and endurance. Beware: As the event winds down and the victorious king takes his celebration lap, an evil wizard, Mordred, attacks, dampening the festivities and threatening to throw the world of Avalon into an age of fire and shadow.

Kingdoms clash, beasts attack and the fire of combat burns bright. Arthur is mortally wounded, but before he dies, he asks his son (the show takes some artistic license with the original tale) to avenge his death.

Fun Dungeon

If you trade in your horse for a ride on an escalator, you'll find yourself in Excalibur's dungeon realms, wandering a fantasy bazaar of games, shops and food counters. A stage area offers free shows, including puppetry, music, storytelling and juggling. And there is always SpongeBob 4D EFX Ride to amuse cranky kids.

The Lion Habitat★

At MGM Grand, 3799 Las Vegas Blvd. S. 877-880-0880. www.mgmgrand.com. Open year-round daily 11am–10pm. Free.

Las Vegas may not have a zoo, but it certainly has its share of lions. The three-story Lion Habitat at MGM Grand houses a variety of African lions and cubs, including Goldie, Metro and Baby Lion. You'll see the big cats from all angles in the glass-enclosed 5,345-square-foot structure, as you walk through the see-through tunnel that runs through the habitat. And it's all free of charge.

The Secret Garden of Siegfried & Roy★

At The Mirage, 3400 Las Vegas Blvd. S. 702-791-7111 or 800-627-6667. www.themirage.com. Open year-round daily Mon–Fri 11am–5:30pm, weekends 10am–5:30pm. $15 adults, $10 children (ages 4-12).

You'll think you're in the jungle when you enter this lush 15-acre refuge, complete with palm trees, flowers, waterfalls and the calls of exotic birds and jungle drums playing in the background. Here you'll find Royal white tigers, white lions, Bengal tigers, snow leopards and more.

Adjoining the garden is the **Dolphin Habitat**, featuring four connecting pools with a sand bottom and an artificial reef. These simulate the natural environment for a group of dolphins that reside here. You can tour the habitat, which provides a sanctuary for Atlantic bottlenose dolphins and also serves as a breeding facility, to watch trainers interact with the gentle mammals.

To truly indulge those flipper fantasies, kids can tap into Mirage's **Dolphin Trainer for a Day** program. It's a hands-on experience of learning about this fascinating creature through the Dolphin Habitat. Participants don wet suits and jump in the water with the trainers and dolphins for some photos and bottle-nosed kisses after they have learned all the hand-signals and spent time getting to know their designated dolphin. The experience takes about six hours and comes with a gourmet lunch. Group sizes are limited. The program costs $500 per person. *Reservations must be made well in advance or through the Mirage concierge desk.*

Feeding Frenzy at Atlantis Aquarium

At The Forum Shops at Caesars Palace, 3570 Las Vegas Blvd. S. 702-893-3807. Tours daily at 1:15pm & 5:15pm. www.robertwynn.com/FishAq.htm.

More than 500 individual fish representing some 100 different species call this 50,000-gallon aquarium home. Make sure you drop by at 3:15pm or 7:15pm, when you can watch divers enter the tank and feed the sharks, rays and other denizens of the deep. The aquarium also offers a below-the-scenes tour of the support facilities during the week. *Dive shows and tours are free of charge.*

Fish Stories at Silverton

3333 Blue Diamond Rd. 702-263-7777 or 866-946-4373. www.silvertoncasino.com.

Silverton's 117,000-gallon inner reef is home to more than 4,000

exotic fish, including stingrays and sharks. A marine biologist feeds them thrice daily *(1:30pm, 4:30pm and 7:30pm)* as he talks to the audience from inside the tank. Check out the Mermaid Lounge for a mesmerizing moment with jellyfish.

Pole Position Raceway

4175 South Arville, 702-227-7223. www.polepositionraceway.com. Adult races: $25 per race; Children: $22.

Put Junior's go-kart fantasies on steroids at Pole Position. This quarter-mile, Euro-inspired indoor track just west of The Strip features electric EK20, 18-horsepower go-karts that kick. The track winds through the 60,000 square foot facility supporting some 58 go-karts in all, racing each other for time relays and reporting results in blazing lights on the wall. Each racer's speed is tracked as they careen and bump at top speeds of 45mph. No wreckages here, just a rollicking good time.

Atlantis Aquarium

MUST DO

Pole Position Raceway

Bob Brye/Las Vegas News Bureau

Wild Rides at Primm

*Primm Valley Resorts, 31900
Las Vegas Blvd. S., Primm
702-386-7867 or 1-800-FUN-STOP.
Open Mon–Fri noon–8pm, Fri–Sat
10am–midnight, Sun 10am–10pm.
Six attractions range from
$5-$8 per ride.
www.primmvalleyresorts.com.*

This resort at the California border with Nevada is actually three casino hotels: Buffalo Bill's, Primm Valley, and Whiskey Pete's. They are all connected by a monorail running between the properties.

Hailing from the days when Vegas promoters pictured the city as a family kind of town, Primm Valley Resorts grabbed the flag and put kids on coasters, drops, and all sorts of rides that only a child can love. Starting with the **Desperado**, Primm has amusement and thrill attractions, three hotel casinos, as well as shopping, golf and entertainment just 40 minutes south of the city.

The **Desperado** is still one of the top thrill rides around town and ranks among the top ten in the country for height and speed. It climbs to an altitude of 209 feet,

tops speeds of 80mph, delivers more than 5 Gs and lasts a heart-pounding 2.43 minutes with nine moments of total weightlessness. A ride requires riders be at least 48 inches tall.

Then there's the **Turbo Drop** that flies into the face of gravity rather than away from it. It's a plunge straight down, from 170 feet in the air, at an intense 45mph and lasts about a minute—45 seconds to climb and 15 seconds, which feel like an hour, to shoot back down. The Adventure Canyon Log Flume continues the action with swirling rapids and treacherous waterfalls inside a Wild West scenario. Riders shoot laser guns at targets and bad guys as they fly by for a moment of marksmanship as well as exhilaration. The ride lasts four minutes.

The Vault is there for those who want to take their dares from the safety of their chairs.

Viewers can choose from different experiences and move through them in a 3-D High Def Digital projection motion simulator ride that is the state of the art for the technology these days.

FOR KIDS

113

SHOPPING

Like everything else in Las Vegas, the city has taken a favored pastime and turned it gold. Shopping is not about finding a blouse or that perfect pair of shoes. It is about passing into a sort of twilight browsers' zone where store merchandise is just a sideline to the real entertainment to be found amid opera trios performing in **St. Mark's Square**, flirtations with buff Roman sentries on the Appian Way, mehndi tattoos offered in Moorish courtyards, or coffee overlooking a catwalk of swaggering fashion models. Shops in Las Vegas see 50,000 people stroll by each day to catch the mall-made action along fantastical promenades ranging from 500,000 to nearly two million square feet. So it is no surprise that shopping has taken its place high on the list of top reasons people visit Las Vegas—just under "pleasure."

The Forum Shops at Caesars Palace

At Caesars Palace, 3570 Las Vegas Blvd. S. 702-893-4800. www.caesars.com/Caesars/ LasVegas.

It's said that all roads lead to Rome. If the foot traffic in The Forum Shops is any indication, that adage rings true. With more than 160 stores, the 675,000-square-foot mall attracts as many as 200,000 visitors on a busy day. No wonder it's billed as the most successful shopping center in the country in terms of sales volume per square foot. The merchandise mix offers everything from high fashion to novelty items. From Longchamp to Fendi and from Anthropologie to Escada, the Forum Shops is one of the wonders of Las Vegas. The

The Forum Shops

Caesars Entertainment

Amen Wardy Home Store features an unusual selection of items for the home. Estee Lauder allows customers to experiment on their own with a full line of make-up.

More Roads to Rome

Forum Shops grew another mini-city in 2004. The ornate, three-tiered extension added to the collection of upscale specialty stores and restaurants with Varvatos, Bruno Magli and Longchamp. The unusual centerpiece here is the circular escalator, but that takes a back seat to the facades of ancient Rome that line the lengthy promenades and the animated statuary and special effects that come to life each hour at otherwise sleepy Forum fountains.

MUST DO

Miracle Mile★

Surrounding (and connected to) Planet Hollywood, 3663 Las Vegas Blvd. S. 702-866-0710 or 888-800-8284. www.miraclemileshopslv.com.

What could be more fitting than a Miracle Mile of shopping encircling Planet Hollywood. For joggers and power walkers, the mall is, indeed, an entertaining mile of merchandise—many purposely ensconced in this location because of their Los Angeles links or affiliations. Stores such as Sur La Table, Swarovski, Tommy Bahama, BCBG, Bettie Page have found a fun home in Las Vegas next to the hippest new hotel on The Strip. Some interesting kiosks and stores remain from the mall's original incarnation as the Desert Passage, which made it a Disneyesque experience of ancient Arabia amid faux medinas and interior desert landscape designs.
You can still find rug merchants and mehndi artists and fine art boutiques among the chains. Restaurants provide all manner of choices from sushi buffets to oyster bars to cheeseburger heaven. Browsers can also stop for a full body massage by hydrojets

Mai Oh Mai

Trader Vic's tore down its legendary Beverly Hills tiki hut location in April 2007 and opened up at the Miracle Mile in June. The 1955 grass hut landmark may be gone from LA but the Mai Tai lives on. The sweet, refreshing rum cocktail was created by Victor Jules "Trader Vic" Bergeron in 1944 and introduced to the Hawaiian islands in the 1950s. Tahitian for "the very best," Mai Tai became the slogan for his entire operation, which eventually grew to number 29 Polynesian-themed restaurants around the world.

($10 for 15 minutes), backrubs by shiatsu chairs ($1 for three minutes) and real time advice (free!) by the wise manager who moonlights as a physiotherapist and kung fu teacher at Zen Zone.
The V Theater has more than a dozen shows, from magic to music, scheduled throughout the days of the week and that does not include the daily Striptease and Pole Dancing classes you can take to learn some new moves and exercise routines.

Miracle Mile Shops

Miracle Mile Shops

🛍 Grand Canal Shoppes

At The Venetian, 3355 Las Vegas Blvd. S. 702-414-1000 or 877-883-6423. www.venetian.com.

Pigeons are all that's needed to make this Venice shopping experience feel any more real (the birds are there, but luckily they're outside the hotel).

Strolling down the cobblestone walkways of this 500,000-square-foot indoor mall at the Venetian, along nearly a quarter-mile of Venice's famed Grand Canal, you'll find more than 70 stores and boutiques. Many of the Grand Canal Shoppes have premiered here for the first time in the US.

At St. Mark's Square (where the pigeons are found in the real Venice), you can take a 15-minute gondola ride down the 1,200-foot-long **Grand Canal** and be serenaded by a gondolier. Even if you skip the gondola ride, the shopping is a trip in itself. Be sure to visit Il Prato, which carries collectible masks and fine paper goods (including colorful glass-point fountain pens), and Ripa de

Over the Top

Looking for luxury in Las Vegas? The Shoppes at Palazzo take high end spending to a new level with 450,000 square feet of uber-designer shopping anchored by the city's first Barneys New York. Manolo Blahnik, Jimmy Choo, Stella McCartney, True Religion—60 international shops. It all connects to the Canal Shoppes for a million square feet of upscale shopping.

Monti, which offers Venetian glass and collectibles.

Another must-see is Sephora, a 10,000-square-foot beauty emporium dedicated to women's perfumes and cosmetics.

Lladro, Tolstoys and Ancient Creations are also fun to browse for gifts. Fine cafés and restaurants, many with canalside seating, are located in this retail area.

As in Europe you can have your pick of gelatos here. Enjoy the flavors of Venice in the flurry of St. Mark's Square.

Grand Canal Shoppes

Fashion Show Mall

🛍 Fashion Show Mall

3200 Las Vegas Blvd. S., at the intersection of Las Vegas Blvd. & Spring Mountain Rd., across from Wynn Las Vegas. 702-369-8382. www.thefashionshow.com.

Whoever said that "bigger is better" must have seen the new Fashion Show Mall.

The first mall to open on The Strip, the venue holds the distinction of being not only its largest shopping establishment but, thanks to a recent expansion, one of the largest shopping centers in the nation. In 2006, the premier retail venue completed a four-year, $1-billion redevelopment, which more than doubled its size to approximately two million square feet.

The renovation included expanded flagship department stores from Neiman-Marcus and Macy's, along with new stores from Saks Fifth Avenue, a prototype

Bridge to the Mall

The Fashion Show connects to Wynn Las Vegas and Encore by a convenient bridge across Las Vegas Boulevard. Those staying At the Wynn properties who want to enhance their shopping time while in Las Vegas can call upon Wynn's own on-staff professional shoppers to do the honors. Sit by the pool, sip those mojitos and wait for the bags to flow in.

Bloomingdale's Home and Nevada's first Nordstrom. It is expected that ultimately the mall will be anchored by eight major department stores. Find the Apple Store here, and the only tapas restaurant in town with a view of The Strip.

On warm days, the 480-foot "cloud" structure above a 72,000-square-foot plaza on The Strip comes in handy for its shade.

Wynn Esplanade

Several designer digs have made their exclusive Las Vegas debut. At **Wynn Esplanade**, off the hotel's main entrance (*see Casinos*). These include Oscar de la Renta, Manolo Blahnik (the only store outside New York), and Graff Diamonds of London (their second US location).

Making Scents

La Vogue boutique features handbags, lacy lingerie and French perfumes, including Paris Las Vegas' own signature fragrance, C'est Si Bon. You can also buy this fragrance in La Menagerie de Paris, which carries fashionable Paris Las Vegas logo merchandise.

At night it presents multimedia fashion images and projections of live fashion shows. Snackers can dine at the 1,500-seat food court or try the California Pizza Kitchen, the Café at Nordstrom or Mariposa at Neiman Marcus hidden away between the more than 200 boutiques and stores.

The mall hosts regular fashion shows on its catwalk area, often sponsored by tenant stores and featuring a charity angle.

Le Boulevard

At Paris Las Vegas, 3655 Las Vegas Blvd. S. 702-946-7000 or 800-634-3434. www.parislv.com.

Le Boulevard cries out from every storefront, Vive la différence!

Le Boulevard

Las Vegas News Bureau

The distinct French flavor is immediately apparent when you enter this 31,000-square-foot retail space that connects Paris to its sister resort, Bally's, beginning at one casino and ending at the other. This French connection is called Le Boulevard and consists of authentic French boutiques in a chic simulated Parisian setting. Find unusual stores here with French accents and items you might otherwise see on the Champs Elyseés.

Crystals

At CityCenter, 3720 Las Vegas Blvd. S. 702-590-9299. www.crystalsatcitycenter.com.

Creators Daniel Libeskind and David Rockwell described it as a living thing, a New York neighborhood unfolding or a scene in nature moving with the diurnal rhythms. Whatever Crystals is, it is a pod-like Mobia strip on the outside and all upscale shopping and art in the inside.

The 500,000 square-foot form of sweeping white spaces, aluminum, glass and wood presents a balancing effect for such stores as Tiffany—a two-level retail spread here and one of the largest in the chain, with a door that opens onto The Strip. Louis Vuitton placed the largest store in North America inside Crystals. Tom Ford has a signature here.

Eva Longoria Parker has a restaurant and nightclub right across from the pub Todd English created. You can even find what might be the one of the only bookstores on The Strip here, too: Assouline by Assouline Publishing, for, say, offbeat books about Barbie.

Crystals

Darrin Bush/Las Vegas News Bureau

🛍 Premium Outlets

875 South Grand Central Parkway.
702-474-7500. 7400.
Las Vegas Blvd. S. 702-896-5599.
www.premiumoutlets.com/
lasvegas/.

If you think Vegas is all about the bargain, you will find them here: at Premium Outlets South near Town Square and North just blocks from Downtown. You secure your Coach and DNKY specials here but you'll also find in season Kate Spade for a third off the normal price, ditto for St. John, even Bose. There are 140 stores at the North site, an outdoor promenade of shops, cooled in summer by misters. The South outlet is indoors and anchored by Saks Off Fifth.

🛍 Town Square

6605 S. Las Vegas Blvd. S
702-269-5000.
mytownsquarelasvegas.com.

If there is something like a destination shopping, dining, entertainment, working, loafing and browsing site in Las Vegas, Town Square is it. Conceived as more of a living space than simply a shopping place, the 117-acre

Time for Their Encore

Encore offers a dozen stores and most of them you won't find anywhere else. Consider Ensemble. Trendy, upmarket, even classy could be used describe the duds in here but ask around and you'll learn about the historic Jackie-O dresses in the back. Real dresses designed for and worn by the former First Lady bearing such labels as Pucci and Givenchy are available for about $4,000 each.

outdoor mega-mall may come as close to an old fashioned town as it gets in Las Vegas. "Neighborhoods" run in themed blocks of Tuscany, Old Mexico and Colonial facades with offices above that look onto the "street" below. Ground floor tenants comprise the nearly 200 shops, restaurants, clubs and entertainment venues. Apple is here; Tommy Bahama's has a flagship here, there is even a Borders here—the only one on The Strip and spared from closing so far. A cute central area for kids offers a park setting with all manner of creative structures for exploration and play.

SHOPPING

NIGHTLIFE

If Las Vegas has anything, it has nightlife. Call it all-night life. Clubs in this town do not get going until at least 11pm and when they do the action often lasts until 4am. Don't be surprised if you encounter a velvet rope or two on your club jaunts.

This is the land of the "ultra lounge" where model wannabes in slinky dark dresses serve $1,000 bottles of champagne, where you have to plunk down a Platinum Card before you find a seat and to get anywhere near that seat you might have to let go of a C-note or two. But Vegas will show you a good time in return with special effects creating dizzying images on the dance floor, wowing pool scenes, plenty of celebrity appeal and a cocktail culture that proffers $3,000 drinks accessorized by diamond-studded straws. If it is scene you want, it is scene you will get. And this scene is like no other.

Chateau

At Paris Las Vegas.3655 Las Vegas Blvd S. 702-776-7770. www.chateaunightclublv.com. Open Tue, Fri and Sat 10pm–4am.

The Chateau's theme evokes the European vibrancy of Paris with modern twists of an old world theme: brushes of indulgent golds, lots of black and hints of rouge just

wants to make you shout *Let Them Eat Cake!* Chrystal Chandeliers spare no reflection as they hang throughout the main room. It's a grand setting for a raucus scene that has had as host Charlie Sheen.

Ghost Bar

At The Palms Casino Resort, 4321 W. Flamingo Rd. 702-942-7777 or 866-725-6773. www.palms.com. Open daily 8pm until late.

Billing itself as "the ultimate apparition," the Ghost Bar at the Palms is a sultry and sophisticated indoor-outdoor lounge and skydeck on the 55th floor of the hotel with a spectacular 360-degree view of Las Vegas. You may have a close encounter of the celebrity kind here: The long list of notables that have visited the Ghost Bar includes Heather Locklear, Carmen Electra, Don Johnson and Nicolas Cage. If celebrity sightings aren't exciting enough for you, try the glass inset in the floor of the skydeck, which offers a jaw-dropping, straight-down view. The 8,000-square-foot

---

Word on Wine

Las Vegas is fast becoming known for its magnificent wine collections. The **Wine Cellar** at **Rio** has a 50,000-bottle collection that includes such rare vintages as a c.1800 Madeira from Thomas Jefferson's cellar, a prize bottle of 1924 Château Mouton Rothschild, and the world's largest selection of Chateau d'Yquem, valued at $2 million. You can taste more than 100 wines by the glass here or simply watch the glass—**Aureole** at Mandalay Bay has a four-story, glass wine tower where tethered "wine angels," scale and pull from the 10,000-bottle collection.

venue has a 30-foot ghost-shaped soffit in the ceiling, which changes colors as a DJ spins a mix of music. Floor-to-ceiling windows and custom, ultra-contemporary lounge furniture decorate the room. Seek privacy in the intimate seating arrangements or mingle at the terrazzo bar.

Stoney's Rockin' Country

9151 Las Vegas Blvd. S. 702-435-BULL (2855). www.stoneysrockincountry.com.

Vegas being Vegas, even country bars and Texas two-step joints have morphed into a new kind of back-at-the-ranch experience: the Cowboy Ultra-Lounge. Stoney's Rockin' Country, runs Tuesdays through Saturdays with doors opening at 7pm. Dance lessons start at 7:30.
The 20,000-square-foot nightclub can fit 1,000 people and has a dance floor the size of a barn, plus the requisite mechanical bull, coin-op pool tables, two full-service bars, a cowboy arcade, a three-lane bowling alley, a $250,000 sound system, go-go girls

I'll Have One of Those
The Ghost Bar's signature **Ghostini** cocktail blends Absolut vodka, Midori and sour mix.

and a VIP ultra-lounge for cowboys with discerning tastes. It also has ladies nights, $10 all-you-can-drink draught and Free Beer Fridays.

JET Nightclub

At The Mirage, 3400 Las Vegas Blvd. S. 702-791-7111 or 800-627-6667. www.jetlv.com. Open Fri, Sat & Mon 10:30pm–4:30am.

Jet features a one-of-a-kind light and laser grid, state-of-the-art cryogenic-effects systems, and what the owners tout as the best sound-design technology available. Three distinct rooms each has its own dance floor, DJ booth and sound system. The main room presents a mix of rock, hip-hop, and popular dance music. A second room is dedicated to house music spun by international DJs, while in the third room you can hear an eclectic mix of music spanning the decades from the early years of rock through the 1980s.

JET Nightclub

MGM Resorts International

Four full-service bars offer specialty cocktails, and the Light group's signature (and pricey) European bottle service is featured in each room of the club.

Pure

At Caesars Palace, 3570 S. Las Vegas Blvd. S. 702-731-7873 or 800-634-6661. www.caesars.com. Open Fri–Sun & Tue 10pm–4am.

Owned by Andre Agassi, Steffi Graf, Shaquille O'Neal and Celine Dion, the 36,000-square-foot nightclub consists of three distinct environments. The main room is draped in shades of snow, cream, egg shell and silver. Three bars here do the mixing beneath a raised VIP area and next to a dance floor surrounded by oversized cushions. Dressed in steamy shades of crimson, the Red Room is reserved for the moneyed crowd, secluded from the main club with its own bar and VIP restrooms. Lush draperies, chandeliers and upholstered walls, and cozy private pods complete the sense of being sequestered. A glass elevator leads up to the Terrace, a 14,000-square-foot hideaway presenting panoramic views of The Strip amid cabanas, tables and a crowded dance floor. A recent addition, the famous Pussycat Dolls Lounge adjoins the larger nightclub, bringing the group's well-noted art of seduction and circumstance to the club. Guests are teased throughout the night by Dolls dropping from the ceiling on swings, swaggering around chairs and props and singing and dancing onstage.

Rain Nightclub

At The Palms Casino Resort, 4321 W. Flamingo Rd. 702-942-7777 or 866-725-6773. www.palms.com. Open Thu 11pm–5am, Fri–Sat 10pm–5am.

If you want to see rain in the desert, you're going to have to go to the Palms. In fact, for a real rainwater experience, try one of the venue's eight water booths, which feature patent-leather banquettes filled with water.
Rain is the ultimate contemporary nightclub and concert venue. It combines performances by international headliners with an electrifying dance club, a private-event facility and intimate enclaves in one dynamic multisensory experience. From the moment you enter through the gold-mirrored mosaic tunnel, which is filled with changing light, fog and sound, you know you're in for a downpour of special effects. Inside, a water wall, a rain curtain, fog, haze and pyrotechnics such as 16-foot fire plumes add to the atmosphere. Luxury, private and VIP accommodations include a cabana level with private cabanas seating eight to 12 guests. Each cabana

Pure

Caesars Entertainment

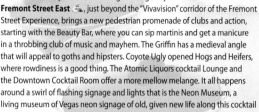

Bring it Downtown

For an unusual experience of the night in Vegas try Downtown. **Fremont Street East** 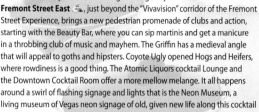, just beyond the "Vivavision" corridor of the Fremont Street Experience, brings a new pedestrian promenade of clubs and action, starting with the Beauty Bar, where you can sip martinis and get a manicure in a throbbing club of music and mayhem. The Griffin has a medieval angle that will appeal to goths and hipsters. Coyote Ugly opened Hogs and Heifers, where rowdiness is a good thing. The Atomic Liquors cocktail Lounge and the Downtown Cocktail Room offer a more mellow melange. It all happens around a swirl of flashing signage and lights that is the Neon Museum, a living museum of Vegas neon signage of old, given new life along this cocktail corridor and blinking all night long.

includes a liquid-crystal display screen, lights that change colors, a mini-bar and specialty furniture. High above the cabanas, six lavish skyboxes boast private balconies overlooking the nightclub below.

Posh

3525 W. Russell Rd.
702-673-1700.
www.poshlasvegas.com.
Open Fri-Sat, midnight until 6am.

It doesn't get sexier than Posh, one of the latest Las Vegas late night scenes to open, this time adjacent to Crazy Horse III Gentleman's Club. It's all part of the Playground, a new concept in all-night entertainment, which includes fresh sushi at Sushi All Night and relaxing puffs at Hookah Lounge.
Call it ground zero for adult partying, a complex of places where anyone, from Shy Sally to the G.I. Jane can find a spot in the wee hours of any morning. The 3,500 square-foot venue offers multiple rooms to satisfy the 24-hour cravings of night wanderers, with kitschy Gothic interiors of Roman columns, oversized mirrors, and dripping chandeliers amid accents of red and black.

It's a world in its own right, intimately designed for a lush and sophisticated night out. From midnight to 2 a.m., ladies enjoy an open bar and free admission, (usually $20-$30) in sound-packed surrounds of top 40, house and R&B tunes while body-painted go-go and sexy peepshow girls perform their moves on surfaces and stages. Bottle service starts at a mere $375.

Lucky Strike Lanes

At Rio, 3700 W. Flamingo Rd.
702-777-7999.
www.riolasvegas.com.
Open Mon–Fri 2pm–3am, Sat &
Sun 11am–3am. Patrons must be
over 21 after 9pm.

Lucky Strike puts a new spin on grandpa's game. Don't expect to rent a lane for $25 and throw in the bowling shoes for $5. The velvet rope comes out at night, the dress code is definitely R to X and the games are hot hot hot.
You can toast your ten-pin strike with Dom Perignon and those hard plastic chairs are soft, plush leather here. Chances are you'll be playing with strangers by the end of the night, no matter who's keeping score.

Studio 54

At MGM Grand, 3799 Las Vegas Blvd. S. 702-891-7279 or 800-929-1111. www.studio54lv.com. Open Tue–Sat 10pm until late.

A high-energy trend-setting nightclub, Studio 54, named for the late, great New York City venue, claims to feature the most eclectic music mix in the country, combined with state-of-the-art sound, lighting and staging. Music, courtesy of a DJ, ranges from cutting-edge sounds to the songs of the 1970s that made the original Studio 54 the epicenter of pop culture and style.

The 22,000-square-foot nightclub offers four dance floors and bars, an exclusive area on the second floor for invited guests, as well as several semi-private lounges.

If you're lucky, you might see one of the surprise acts (in the past these have included the Go-Gos and Prince) that take the stage on any given evening.

Studio 54

Robert Brye/Las Vegas News Bureau

Tabu

At MGM Grand, 3799 Las Vegas Blvd. S. 702-891-7816 or 800-929-1111. www.mgmgrand.com. Open Tue–Sun 10pm until dawn.

Symbolizing everything chic, cosmopolitan and innovative, Tabu's design is a distinct combination of modern fashion and refined style. A comfortable level of vocals allows guests to carry on conversations while taking in the scene and enjoying a cocktail.

Although there's no dance floor, guests have been known to boogie on the 700-pound concrete tables—which, as luck would have it, house projected imagery systems that react to motion. That makes for quite an interactive scene. Just laying a glass down on the table causes the under-lying image on the table to change.

Three distinct rooms here cater to every mood. The main room with its reactive tables has a large bar and a DJ booth. In the back of the club, the discreet Champagne Bar is decorated with a cool animated mural of the desert.

You can reserve the circular Tantra Room, with its own bar and black marble floor, for private parties.

Christian Audigier

At TI, 3300 Las Vegas Blvd. S. 702-466-9723 or 800-944-7444. www.audigierlv.com. Open Thu–Sun 10pm until dawn.

Part tattoo parlor, part South Beach sheen, the new Christian Audigier night scene at TI does not cast even a sliver of orange in the shadows of the space formerly known as Tangerine. That's because Audigier,

Tao

Las Vegas News Bureau

the heretofore French clothing designer of Melrose Avenue in Hollywood, puts the Ed Hardy, "skull and roses" tattoo art of his clothing brands all over the new Strip scene spot.

It's a Goth world inside—silver skulls looming over the shiny black faux croc leather banquettes, backed by heavy vermillion velvet drapery that one might find in a haunted house or, say, a cathouse, all dramatically offset by two illuminated 1,000-gallon tanks full of jellyfish

Outside, the patio setting over the Pirate's Cove is all white with plush cushions, clean lines, patio attire you might find in finer homes. But the seats are some of the hottest on The Strip.

Audigier's label-mania extends to libations with his own lines of wines from vineyards in the South of France. As with most ultra-lounges in Las Vegas, you won't sit unless you pay the price, usually a C-note or three … for a bottle.

Tao

At The Venetian, 3355 Las Vegas Blvd. S. 702-388-8338 or 877-283-6423. www.venetian.com. Open Thu–Sat 10:30pm–5:30am.

Los Angeles glitterati favor this 40,000-square-foot "Asian City," a multifaceted and multistory venue housing a restaurant, an ultra-lounge and a nightclub. Among the highlights of the $20-million, Zen-like dining and entertainment complex are an outside terrace with Strip views. It has two rooms: The Temple and The Emperors Ballroom, each with its own varied music format; eight private sky boxes with mini-bars, espresso machines, and banquettes outfitted with secure purse drawers. Then there's the European bottle service, and state-of-the-art everything—from lighting to sound to multimedia projection. A chic ultra-lounge serves as a gathering spot for cocktails and conversation, while the 10,000-square-foot Tao Nightclub pulses with energy. Summers get a boost from the heat with pool cabana service at night for those who want to shell out a grand for sitting and service.

SPAS

If you can't take the heat of Las Vegas go for the steam in one of its posh, over-the-top spas. In these veritable pampering palaces you can have your feng shui adjusted, your dosha doused, face your primal past ... or simply follow your bliss. Here's the rub.

Aqua Sulis

At JW Marriott Las Vegas Resort & Spa, 221 N. Rampart Blvd.
702-869-7777 or 877-869-8777.
www.marriott.com.

Set in a scenic desert sanctuary 20 minutes away from The Strip (next to Red Rock National Preserve), Aqua Sulis fosters an indoor/outdoor experience focusing on the healing powers of water. Prepare for your treatment by hitting the soak and plunge pools—especially refreshing in the hot summer months—that line a landscaped patio area outside the 40,000-square-foot spa. The battery of hot soaks, cold soaks, jets that nail nearly every muscle in your body, and a menu of treatments that run from European to exotic make coming here well worth the trip. Energized spa-goers can hit the gym, where two-story floor-to-ceiling windows overlook the pool and desert, or take advantage of Tai Chi, Pilates and yoga classes.

Aqua Sulis

© GaryKufner/Marriott International

Canyon Ranch SpaClub at The Venetian

3355 Las Vegas Blvd. S.
702-414-3600 or 877-220-2688.
www.canyonranch.com.

Meanwhile, back at the ranch, Canyon Ranch at The Venetian to be precise, the well-known name in health resorts is welcoming people to their first SpaClub in Las Vegas. This peaceful and plush facility offers more than 120 spa services. It also features a fitness facility with a wellness center staffed by physicians and nutritionists. Canyon Ranch Salon *(4th floor)* offers a full list of beauty services from haircuts to full makeovers. With the opening of Palazzo adjacent to the Venetian, the Canyon Ranch facility connects the two properties with an added 65,000 square feet of pure pleasure space to become the largest hotel spa in Las Vegas, if not the US.

Spa & Salon Bellagio

3600 La Vegas Blvd. S.
702-694-7444 or 888-987-6667.
www.bellagio.com.

Spa & Salon Bellagio has been a long time coming. The resort that changed the face of Las Vegas when it opened in 1998 has done it again—this time with a new 65,000-square-foot spa that counts 56 treatment rooms and 12 skin-care rooms, making it the largest pampering palace in town to date.

Located in the recent 33-story tower addition, the spa sports an elegant design with clean lines, the colors of natural stone and private candlelit places to meditate. You'll find reflecting pools and waterwalls throughout, and an infusion of cool jades and hand-blown glass in the calming spaces. A private Watsu pool room allows for the special namesake stretching treatment that simulates being back in the womb.

For the ultimate in opulence, the Egyptian Gold treatment leaves the body exfoliated, moisturized and glowing with a dusting of real gold.

🌿 Qua Spa at Caesars Palace

3570 Las Vegas Blvd. S. 702-731-7110 or 800-634-6661. www.harrahs.com/casinos/caesars-palace.

The sybaritic pleasures to be found here along the second floor of the new Augustus Tower take time to assimilate. And time is what you need here, to soak in the mineral-infused waters of the indoor cleansing pools: the Tepidarium, Caldarium and Frigidarium calibrated at 98, 104 and 72°F. Water jets and deluge showers hit the muscles and calm the nerves. Treatments range from herb garden oil massages to Swarovrski crystal treatments that keep the body in sparkle for five days. Complement your massage with a sweaty sit in the sauna followed by a frozen few moments in the spa's arctic chamber, where snow blows in the purple-silver glow. Top it off with a choice of tea, attended to by the spa's tea concierge.

Arctic Ice Room, Qua Spa

Caesars Entertainment

The Spas at CityCenter

3780 Las Vegas Blvd. S. 702-590-7757. www.citycenter.com.

CityCenter presents three notable and distinctive spas within a single campus of design-forward properties. 🌿 **Spa Aria**, Spa Vdara and the 🌿 **Spa at Mandarin Oriental** each offer completely different experiences, according to the hotel to which they are attached. Vdara, a green and ecologically-themed condohotel offers a top to bottom organic and holistic immersion as the central focus of treatments and ambience. Spa Aria is a sprawling affair to match the Aria Hotel, which is the only "Vegas-sized" property at CityCenter. The Spa brings some unusual complimentary components: a salt room where you can lie on zero-gravity loungers where music syncs to the electric massage vibrations. It also has a heated granite room where 15 minutes on a heated flat slab will leach any lingering toxins from the body and step up the

SPAS

internal cell vibration. Finally, the Spa at Mandarin Oriental offers such conveniences as dawn yoga sessions and heated stone lounge chairs by a floor to ceiling window over The Strip.

🧖 The Spa at Wynn Las Vegas

3131 Las Vegas Blvd. S.
702-770-7000 or 888-320-7123.
www.wynnlasvegas.com.

In addition to nearly 50 treatment rooms, the Spa offers a spacious Jacuzzi flanked by cool plunge pools, two "deluge" chambers where powerful water columns pound out sore muscles on tired shoulder and neck areas; a waiting area by a fire that seems to spring from a flood of glistening rock crystals and a large coed waiting room/Zen chamber between the men's and women's area paneled in faux Indian carved stone, with soothing fountains amid stands of bamboo. Some unusual offerings for treatments here include the Arabian Massage, an 80-minute

session of warm oils massaged into powerful pressure point areas in the scalp and feet, as well as an all-over body massage.

🧖 The Spa at Trump

702-982-0000 or 877-878-6711.
www.trumplasvegashotel.com.

Although this spa is not bathed in gold, it infuses jewels into every touch. The Spa at Trump is the only spa on The Strip so far to use Shiffa, a product line out of Dubai that infuses precious oils with the powers of diamonds, emeralds, rubies and sapphires. Clients choose their stone according to their desired state: diamonds for clarity and enlightenment; Emeralds for harmony; Rubies for revitalization and Emeralds for healing and intuition. Facsimiles of the stones are placed about the room and the therapist then rubs elixirs paired with the gem of choice into the client's skin with a deep, heated massage.

Another first for Vegas—guests will find the city's only Kate Somerville facials available there, in fact the only spot you can currently find them outside of West Hollywood. Meticulously trained therapists consult with patients and then produce the secrets that have hooked a Hollywood following. Among the options—an intensified LED light that beams deep into cells to produce healthy collagens.The healing element of The Spa at Trump continues in the relaxation room with teas and healthy snacks (antioxidant gummy bears anyone?) and spritzes from Sprayology, which uses homeopathic principles to calm, rejuvenate, fix travel stress

The Spa at Wynn Las Vegas

© Bettie Miner/Wynn Las Vegas

and even combat hot flushes. Helpful "spa attaches" assist with any need, from blending teas to preparing iPod selections. Beauty services extend beyond nails and hair to 15-minute teeth whitening, even shaving. Men can have a full shaving session using Bali-based Hommage herbal products. Healthy cuisine is available at H2(eau) overlooking the pool area. Choose power smoothies and elixirs for a meal in a drink. A quiet lap pool for soaking and sunning is just outside and makes a good place to rest after a treatment, or for a peaceful lunch. The pool is heated for year-round use.

Drift Spa at Palms

4381 W. Flamingo Rd.
702-932-7777 or 866-942-7772.
www.palmsplace.com.

Drift Spa at Palms puts a 50,000-square-foot, two-story, sanctuary of sunlight and design in the Palms new 50-story glass tower just off The Strip.
The spa brings Las Vegas' first true "hammam," a coed Turkish bath, that is traditionally a place to detox and relax while catching up on the local gossip. If the desert sun doesn't do the job, guests can bronze up in the spa's Sunset Tan wing and complete their 'E!" moment with a color-up in Michael Boychuck's salon.
There's a spa access fee of $30 for hotel guests and $35 for non-guests that can be waived with such treatments as the "Rockin' Desert Quench," an 80-minute time-stopper that starts with envelopment in warmed agave nectar, followed by a desert body buff made from crushed desert

plants and flowers, a massage with warmed basalt stones, and then a desert aloe wrap, topped with desert flowers body butter.

Spa at Red Rock Resort

11011 W. Charleston Blvd.
702-797.7777 or 866-767.7773.
www.redrocklasvegas.com.

Guests can plan an entire vacation around this spa, a resort destination, 20 minutes west of The Strip. Ultra-modern design inspired by the surrounding Red Rock Canyon keeps the spa drenched in rich shades of red with accents of cream and chocolate brown. The Adventure Spa program combines the spa experience with the beauty of nature by packaging pampering with desert adventures.
A secluded pool area adds sanctuary and soaking to this high desert escape. If the city is not electric enough for you, amp up with an Espresso Scrub or Espresso Anti-cellulite Wrap. Or take it down a notch with a professional Reiki session.

Well Spa at Platinum

211 E. Flamingo Rd.
702-365-5000 or 877-211-9211.
www.theplatinumhotel.com.

The Platinum's tiny and compact Well Spa offers a swell of soft blue and green hues to soothe and comfort and plenty of corners and cubbies within which to retreat between treatments.
Especially lovely are chaises surrounded by gossamer veils for privacy, with blankets, teas and fruits within reach.

RESTAURANTS

The venues listed below were selected for their ambience, location and/or value for money. Rates indicate the average cost of an appetizer, a main and a dessert for one person (not including tax, gratuity or beverages). Most restaurants are open daily and accept major credit cards. Call for information regarding reservations, dress code and opening hours. For a list of restaurants by theme, *see p144*. **The Michelin Guide** has more recommended restaurants.

| *Luxury* | **$$$$** over $100 | *Moderate* | **$$** $25–$50 |
| *Expensive* | **$$$** $50–$100 | *Inexpensive* | **$** under $25 |

American Fish

Chef Center/MGM Resorts International

Luxury

 Alize
$$$$ French
*The Palms. 4321 W. Flamingo Rd.
Dinner only. 702-951-7000.
www.andrelv.com.*
You can come for the views—the top floor of the Palms offers all the twinkling and blinking entertainment you could want—or come for the menu that André Rochat has prepared. The recipient of a star this year from Michelin inspectors, Rochat's food includes savory French favorites in his foie gras and escargot presentations and adds those accents to pan seared Muscovy duck breast, pork tenderloin, even peppercorn crusted filet mignon with Cognac cream sauce.

American Fish
$$$$ Regional Seafood
*Aria at CityCenter, 3730 Las Vegas
Blvd. S. Dinner only. 800-230-2742.
www.arialasvegas.com/dining/
american-fish.aspx.*
American Fish gives Michael Mina another outlet in Las Vegas and gives the city a spot in the desert where they know they can get the freshest of seafood catches prepared and brought to their table in four ways: salt-baked, wood-grilled, cast-iron griddled and ocean-water poached. The German chef who primed his knives under Charlie Trotter perfected what he believes are the best treatments for seafood and serves them in a casual, almost family-style restaurant with large booths, crowded tables

and a bustle of activity and noise. Pre-theater three-course dinner menus for $55 per person present such sampling convenience with such choices as sea salt-baked branzino (Mediterranean seabass) with bacon-wrapped potatoes, while a tasting menu for $95 offers seven tapas plates, no choices necessary.

Aureole
$$$$ Contemporary American
Mandalay Bay, 3950 Las Vegas Blvd. S. Dinner only. 702-632-9325 or 800-632-7000. www.aureolelv.com.
Celebrated chef Charlie Palmer brought his New York City restaurant to town in 1999 and it continues to win accolades for both its culinary combinations and wine pairings. Centerpiece of these sprawling, whitewashed and wood interiors is the four-story, stainless-steel and glass wine tower designed by Adam Tihany. "Wine angels," aerialists/wine stewards, will retrieve your preferred vintage among the 10,000 bottles by means of mechanical hoists. The menu ranges from succulent citrus-grilled escolar to a hearty caramelized veal chop. Charlie's onion soup is a fixture with foie gras, truffles and a Gruyère pastry puff. Prix-fixe, three-course tasting menus start at $75, with wine pairings added for $55.

Binion's Steak House
$$$$ Surf & Turf
128 Fremont St. (in Binion's Gambling Hall and Hotel). Dinner only. 702-382-1600. www.binions.com.
This is true old school Vegas, but with a view. Tuxed waiters serve seafood and prime rib on candlelit tables high above the

Wine tower, Aureole

Glenn Pinkerton/Las Vegas News Bureau

city (24 floors, but that was a high rise in mid-century Las Vegas). A pianist adds to the retro romance on weekends. The signature plate is chicken fried lobster, if you dare.

Carnevino
$$$$ Italian Steak
Palazzo, 3325 Las Vegas Blvd. S. 702-789-4141. Lunch and Dinner www.carnevino.com.
Chef Mario Batali and winemaker Joe Bastianich (NYC: Babbo, Otto, Esca. LA: Osteria and Pizzeria Mozza) have partnered up for some food magic at Palazzo in a pricey dining salon that is the perfect place to go to impress the boss, seal the deal or show mom the love. Seattle's Batali, unquestionably the king of carne, took his lessons from Marco Pierre White and three years of intense culinary training in the Northern Italian village of Borgo Capanne. He's collected his share of James Beard awards and authored eight cookbooks. His talents are tested in such dishes as handcut steak tartare Piedmont, pappardelle with "porcini trifolati," and classic, house-aged beef steaks rubbed with sea salts, peppers and fresh rosemary for a slightly charred crust. A $40 three-course, pre-theater menus is available at 5:30.

Bradley Ogden
$$$$ Californian
Caesars Palace, 3570 Las Vegas Blvd. S. Dinner only. 702-731-7413, or 877-346-4642. www.caesars.com.
San Francisco chef Bradley Ogden's signature Las Vegas restaurant is an eye-catcher, right off the lobby of Caesars Palace. Ogden, who gained fame for his culinary creations at the Lark Creek Inn in Marin County, California, creates a new menu daily according to the best seasonal ingredients he can muster. Fresh seems to be the theme of the restaurant and complements the sleek design.

Maytag blue cheese soufflé, Columbia River wild king salmon, and Four Story Farms dry-aged ribeye are just a sampling of what you might find. Want something more casual, less time-consuming and less expensive? Sit at the bar and grab a lighter menu featuring the likes of raw oysters, sandwiches and artisan cheeses.

Le Cirque
$$$$ French
Bellagio. 3600 Las Vegas Blvd. S. Dinner only. 702-693-7111. www.bellagio.com.
Straight from the Maccioni family of New York, Le Cirque has made quite the sensation in Las Vegas and recently earned a Michelin star for its exquisite, bold, transcendent persona. The room is as exciting as the food here—colorful whimsy designed by Adam D. Tihany. Count on creative fusion preparations with French accents such as Szechwan pepper and cardamom roasted salmon, confit vegetables, lobster oil, crustacean jus; rabbit symphony: ravioli, roasted loin, braised leg with crispy spaëtzles,

Riesling sauce; Save room for pastry chef Jaret Blinn's desserts.

Joël Robuchon
$$$$ French
MGM Grand. 3799 Las Vegas Blvd. S. 702-891-7925. Dinner only. www.mgmgrand.com/
It's not often one can move through a dining experience and be certain to have "the meal of a life time." Such a moment can be found at Joël Robuchon. The man who claimed the only three-star Michelin rating in Las Vegas requires each dish, from truffle langoustine ravioli to French hen with roasted foie gras to be an oeuvre not unlike a painting just signed by the artist as it goes to table. A 16-course ever-changing degustation menu costs $385 per person. **L'Atelier du Robuchon** offers a taste of what this meal can be for a fraction of the cost in a 40-seat diner next doot.

Sage
$$$$ American Nouvelle
Aria at CityCenter. 3730 Las Vegas Blvd. 877-230-2742. Dinner only. www.arialasvegas.com/dining/sage.aspx.
Where else can you start your dining experience with an absinthe

Foie Gras Custard Brulée, Sage

tasting treatment and end your meal with a hot chocolate flight send-off? Sage is Chicago star, Shawn McClain's, first Las Vegas venture and he is giving it everything he's got for a wowing time from entrance to exit.

The ambience is tasteful French bistro, if not upscale Speakeasy, but with the formal touches that would attract the noblesse. Dining is in a large room where it is possible to hold a quiet conversation across a wide table.

Menu choices bring such options as Wagyu beef tartare—crushed caper aioli, slow poached egg, crispy chocolate; or 48-hour Beef Belly—chestnut purée, fig glaze, celery hearts, and McClain's signature foie gras custard brulée. Most of the bites melt in your mouth and onto your belly.

Restaurant Guy Savoy

$$$$ French Californian
Caesars Palace. 3570 Las Vegas Blvd. S. 702-731-7286. Dinner only. www.guysavoy.com.

Guy Savoy, inventive kitchen maestro of three-Michelin-star fame in Paris, earned two more in Las Vegas in 2008 from for his statements using unsung American ingredients, such as Santa Barbara prawns, Hawaiian pomfret and Long Island oysters and putting them to work with deft simplicity. Find such hits as artichoke and black truffle soup; cardamom duck stuffed with foie gras and glazed chestnuts; and crispy veal sweetbread sandwiches with small potatoes and black truffles.

A "TGV" (named for the French bullet train), 90-minute, four-course taste of Savoy experience runs $190 per person with an added wine program recommendable and at the ready. The $290 per person, ten-course "menu prestige" option makes it a whole evening.

Twist

$$$$ French Eclectic
Mandarin Oriental. 3752 Las Vegas Blvd. S. Dinner only. 702-590-8888. www.mandarinoriental.com/ lasvegas/dining/twist/.

Mandarin Oriental Hotel Group

Sampling the works of a Michelin three-star chef in the US is a rare treat, indeed. Pierre Gagnaire presents this opportunity on the 23rd floor of the Mandarin Oriental – his only US venue. With Twist, Gagnaire introduces an entirely new dining concept that matches flavors and textures in surprising ways: gelée made from Guinness; swordfish ice cream of asparagus scented with cardamom; darphin potato, topped with quenelle of prune pâte. The dinner-only restaurant offers a nightly pre-theater menu, seasonal à la carte offerings, and a lavish six-course tasting experience.

Expensive

CUT
$$$ Steakhouse
Palazzo, 3325 Las Vegas Blvd. S. 702-789-4141. www.palazzo lasvegas.com/cut.aspx.

The 160-seat cruelty-free CUT steakhouse at Palazzo shows its stars through a menu of organically grown ingredients, coddled farm animals and a sustainable food approach from seed to feed to earth-friendly menus. Combining Wolfgang Puck's kitchen wisdom and passion for culinary perfection, CUT earns its chops as possibly the finest steakhouse in Vegas, even if you don't eat steak. The corn-fed, Nebraska-raised and 35-day dry-aged USDA prime cuts, the Japanese Wagyu wedges, and the Kobe short ribs will just about lay you flat on taste alone, but the lobster & crab "Louis" cocktail with spicy tomato-horseradish, and roasted wild French turbot choices could steal the show.

Mesa Grill
$$$ Southwestern
Caesars Palace, 3570 S. Las Vegas Blvd. S. 702-650-5965 or 800-634-6661. www.mesagrill.com.

Celebrity chef Bobby Flay's first restaurant outside New York City, Mesa Grill is located in the Augustus Tower at Caesars Palace, where it earned its first Michelin star. Here, Flay interprets zesty Southwestern cuisine in a high-energy dining room. Between his three New York City restaurants—including the original Mesa Grill—cookbooks, and several shows on the Food TV network, Flay has established himself as a major American culinary force.

For Mesa starters, try the smoked chicken and black bean quesadilla or the goat cheese queso fundido. Then perhaps move on to the coffee-spice-rubbed rotisserie filet mignon, or the blue-corn-crusted red snapper. Flay also has restaurants in the Bahamas, Atlantic City and New Jersey.

Michael Mina
$$$ Seafood
Bellagio. 3600 Las Vegas Blvd. S. Dinner only. 702-693-7223. www.bellagio.com.

This is one of four restaurants by Michael Mina in Las Vegas but the only one of his venues to earn the coveted Michelin star. Favorites here include the lobster pot pie, the black mussel soufflé, phyllo crumb-crusted Dover sole and the caviar parfait. The setting is upscale business, lots of woods amid glass and leather in a hectic, but well orchestrated, dining space.

miX
$$$ French
THEhotel at Mandalay Bay, 3950 Las Vegas Blvd. S. Dinner only. 702-632-9500. www.chinagrillmgt.com.

If Las Vegas is a city of lights, dinner at the one Michelin star Mix is indeed a sparkling date, under the

miX

glow of the chandelier's 15,000 hand-blown orbs. Here, on the 64th floor of THEhotel, Alain Ducasse's singular dining venture in Vegas sizzles amid a sleek atmosphere of pearly tones and window walls affording spectacular views of The Strip. The acclaimed chef spares no calories to get his customers' approval. Black truffles and foie gras pair well with many dishes, including pressed chicken and beef tenderloin.

Ducasse's version of that comfort-food staple, macaroni and cheese, is made with ham, Gruyère and black truffles. Before or after dinner, head to the bar for some heady views. Even the bathroom offers a window on this world.

The open-air terrace puts you in the clouds.

Nobhill

$$$ Regional American
MGM Grand, 3799 Las Vegas Blvd. S. Dinner only. 702-891-7433. www.mgmgrand.com.

Inspired by the traditional neighborhood restaurants found throughout the San Francisco area, Chef Michael Mina has combined that city's most innovative dishes into a unique menu. The dining room centers on a wood-fired bread oven. Signature dishes such as lobster pot pie and North Beach cioppino are complemented by organic vegetables and greens.

Rao's

$$$ Italian
Caesars Palace. 3570 Las Vegas Blvd. S. Dinner only. 702-731-RAOS. www.raos.com.

You can count the cast members of the Sopranos among the signed photos lining the walls at Rao's, a

Meatballs with pasta, Rao's
© Jonny Miller/Caesars Entertainment

sweet sliver of East Harlem right in the middle of the casino at Caesars Palace. Pasta is served family style with a side of meaty meatballs, the way the 111-year-old original restaurant opposite Jefferson Park on 114th Street always has. Unlike the ten-table New York original you can actually get seated here and get a taste of Frank Pellegrino's legendary chicken with lemon and vinegar, spaghetti with broccoli sauce and seafood salad. No menus are offered. While dining you might be greeted by a member of the Sopranos. The owner, Frank Jr., played the raspy-breathed FBI chief during the series and is the fifth generation of the Rao's family to run the restaurant.

rm seafood

$$$ Seafood
Mandalay Place, 3930 Las Vegas Blvd. S. Dinner only. 702-632-9300. www.rmseafood.com.

Seafood master Rick Moonen closed his acclaimed New York City establishment to put seafood in the desert at Mandalay Place with his vision stamped on every shell and fin. His Las Vegas venture creates a nautical-themed environment of mahogany wood and water, where the freshest of sustainable fish and shellfish make for a succulent

135

dining experience. Whether you choose a tasting menu with perfectly paired wines or an à la carte selection that changes with the seasons and moods of the kitchen, seafood takes on new character here with such creations as wild striped bass with hen of the woods mushrooms and black truffle vinaigrette; abalone with uni butter and Pacific sturgeon caviar; and Mediterranean mussel soufflé in Madras curry butter.

Simon

$$$ Creative Retro
Palms Place. 4381 W. Flamingo Rd. 702-944-3292. BLD. www.simonatpalmsplace.com.
Kerry Simon is one of the pioneers of the Las Vegas star chef scene whose initial venture, an eponymous dining hub at the Hard Rock, virtually launched the rock star-faced culinary maestro into the firmament of cuisine's most notable. A Hyde Park alum who's spent time in such places as The Plaza's Edwardian Room, and with Jean-Georges Vongerichten when he opened Mercer Kitchen in NYC, Simon has found his own sensibilities that extend to sushi, meatloaf and Tandoori arctic char as much as they do to his signature "1960s desserts (homemade Snowballs, anyone?).
Sunday brunch here is the thing. People come for the Bloody Mary bar alone.

StripSteak

$$$ American Steak
Mandalay Bay. 3950 Las Vegas Blvd. S. 702-632-7200. Dinner only. www.mandalaybay.com.
StripSteak is what happens when you get a Las Vegas favorite like Michael Mina to open up a not-your-daddy's steakhouse in one of the hottest hotels in the US. If steak can have a scene, it has one at StripSteak. Catch it on the right night and you might even get hot-pants-clad go-go girls thrown into the meal. Mina makes his mark by infusing the dining scene with technology whether using wood-burning grills or the six circulating, slow-poaching chambers. It's a perfect piece of meat every time, stoked with the subtlest touch of mesquite-infused smokiness. Sides add delicious coronary contraband: fries with dipping sauces, garlic mashed potatoes, tomato-dusted onion rings. Also find true Kumamoto oysters here and Japanese "A5" Kobe steaks.

Julian Serrano

$$-$$$ Spanish
Aria at CityCenter. 3730 Las Vegas Blvd. S. 877-230-2742. Lunch and Dinner. www.arialasvegas.com/ dining/julian-serrano.aspx.
The man who gave Las Vegas Picasso, the city's first five diamond restaurant, is on the scene at Aria cooking up bar-none paellas and tapas treats with all the Catalan earthiness a celebrated and fussy French chef can muster. The concept allows Serrano to go

Tuna raspberry skewer, Julian Serrano

CityCenter/MGM Resorts International

wild, cooking up fancy paisan fare straight from the mountaintop villages of Spain and putting on plates for very affordable prices, considering the resumé of the chef and the nature of the spot. Paellas are the best you'll find in Las Vegas and will easily fill two appetites. There is a special vegetarian menu, too—another rarity in this steak and martini town. Be sure to check out the bathrooms for a speedy lesson in lascivious Spanish phrases.

Moderate

The Bootlegger Bistro
$$ Italian
7700 Las Vegas Blvd. S., between Warm Springs & Blue Diamond Rds. Open 24 hours. 702-736-4939. www.bootleggerlasvegas.com.
For those who want a touch of Las Vegas the way it used to be, the Bootlegger is for you. Owned by Maria and Albert Perri, and their daughter, Lorraine Hunt (former Lt. Gov. of Nevada), this restaurant offers real home-style Italian cooking (Mama Maria comes in three times a week to oversee the making of the sauces, meatballs and sausage) along with great old-fashioned Las Vegas entertainment. On Friday and Saturday nights, Hunt's husband, Blackie, and entertainer Sonny King (Jimmy Durante's partner for 30 years) do a show called *Off The Cuff.*

Bouchon
$$ French
The Venetian, 3355 Las Vegas Blvd. S. 702-414-6200. www.venetian.com.
Thomas Keller, whose new New York City restaurant, Per Se was

Bouchon

The Venetian

recently awarded three Michelin stars, brings his considerable culinary talents to The Venetian at Bouchon. A French pewter bar, a multihued mosaic floor, deep-blue velvet banquettes, antique light fixtures and an expansive hand-painted mural complement the authentic bistro fare here. Breakfast and dinner are served daily; lunch is available on weekends. The seasonal menu offers classics including steak frites, roasted chicken, and trout amandine, bolstered by daily specials. Several items, like croque madame and boudin blanc, are available any time of day.

Brio
$$ Italian
6653 Las Vegas Blvd. S. (in the Las Vegas Town Square Mall). 702-914-9145. www.brioitalian.com.
The thing about this new chain to the Vegas landscape is its location. It's smack in the middle of the new **Town Square Mall**, an open cityscape of decorative small town and European village facades. Brio offers dining and lounging within a spacious outdoor patio within this setting and even keeps a fire pit going for conversation, ambience and warmth. Find all the flavorful Tuscan-inspired cuisine available

RESTAURANTS

137

under the Nevada sun. Leave room for Tiramisu. Consider brunch here on weekends.

Burger Bar
$$ American
Mandalay Bay, 3930 Las Vegas Blvd. S. 702-632-9364.
www.mandalaybay.com.
Decked out with leatherette booths surrounded by warm woods, Hubert Keller's (of Fleur de Lys) hip Burger Bar at **Mandalay Place** has received much attention for serving the most expensive burger in Las Vegas.

The Rossini, for $60, is all Kobe beef, sautéed foie gras and shaved truffles with Madeira sauce, served on an onion bun. But you can build your own more affordable burger (of beef, lamb, turkey or vegetarian) at this upscale eatery for as little as $8.

Choose among more than three dozen toppings—from baby spinach and avocado to Jalapeño bacon and foie gras—for an extra 50¢ to $12. Wash down your meal with a selection from the menu of hand-crafted microbrews.

Japonais
$$ Japanese Fusion
Mirage, 3400 Las Vegas Blvd. S. 702-791-7111.
www.japonaislavegas.com.
The eye-candy interiors by Jeffery Beers are worth the visit alone. But the hot marriage of classic French culinary with precision Japanese preparation begets a dining experience to dazzle the senses with each new creative twist. Try chestnut chicken, Le Quack Japonais, or "The Rock," thinly sliced marinated New York strip cooked on a hot rock right at the table.

Mon Ami Gabi
$$ French
Paris Las Vegas, 3655 Las Vegas Blvd. S. 702-944-4224.
www.monamigabilasvegas.com.
Named for chef Gambino Soletino, this restaurant offers a charming bistro décor that spells 19C-Paris all the way. Its patio dining on The Strip (complete with misters to cool patrons in summer) is one of the best people-watching sites in the city, and a great spot from which to view the Bellagio fountain show. At night, the setting turns romantic with candlelight and bistro classics such as steak frites.

Mon Ami Gabi

Darrin Bush/Las Vegas News Bureau

Sushi Roku

$$ Japanese
3500 Las Vegas Blvd. S.
702-733-7373.
www.sushiroku.com.

This is sushi with a scene, both inside and out. Located in the far reaches of the **Forum Shops** at Caesars, the restaurant features floor-to-ceiling cathedral-sized windows right over some of the most flamboyant neon on The Strip. The place is often in use for bachelor (and bachelorette) parties. Try the Omakasi menu of chef's choice plates. Expect usual dishes to have special touches—yellowtail sashimi with diced chilies, or homemade tofu with white truffles or caviar and lemon.

r bar

$$ Seafood
Mandalay Place, 3930 Las Vegas Blvd. S. 702-632-9300.
www.mandalayplace.com.

Sister to rm seafood, r bar occupies part of the same space. It's located on the ground floor (rm seafood fills the second floor), just off the entrance of **Mandalay Place** as you're coming from the casino. Eat at the stainless-steel bar, in the high-ceilinged dining room, or on the indoor patio.

Pressed for time? Order your meal to-go and head for the pool, your room or wherever. r bar is renowned for its seafood chowders; if you prefer oysters, an oyster-tasting menu offers bivalves fresh from 11 different areas of the Atlantic and Pacific. Chef Rick Moonen practices conscious cuisine, using only caught fish that have a sustainable presence in our oceans, for properly farmed fish and other proteins.

Shibuya

$$ Japanese
MGM Grand, 3799 Las Vegas Blvd. S. Dinner only. 702-891-1111.
www.mgmgrand.com.

The food at Shibuya matches the vibrant urban Tokyo neighborhood from which the restaurant takes its name. The space is divided into three areas that feature sushi, Teppan and à la carte specialties. Complement your entrée with the perfect sake, thanks to Shibuya's sake-pairing program. The room's design captures the essence of fast-paced Tokyo with video screens reflected in mirrored plexiglass above, for a kaleidoscopic effect of constant movement. Master sushi chef Hidebumi Sueyoshi presides over the 50ft marble sushi bar.

Patio, Vintner Grill

Vinter Grill

Vintner Grill, West Las Vegas

**$$ California/
   Mediterranean Fusion**
*10100 W. Charleston Blvd.,
Suite 150. 702-214-5590.*
www.vglasvegas.com.

OK. Madonna dined here. So did Jagger, McCartney, Springsteen, Leno, Streisand, the list goes on. Located in a stripmall business park in Summerlin, some ten miles west of the neon near the JW Marriott and Red Rock Resort, Vintner Grill still packs the Viceroy-style, retro-chic dining room most nights. Chef Matthew Silverman cut his teeth in the kitchens of Wolfgang Puck and by 30 managed to make his mark on the competitive Las Vegas culinary scene with an American-Mediterranean fusion approach that yields such original entrées as crispy calamari with haricot verts, lemon and curry aioli; bistro steak medallions with basmati rice and portabella mushroom cream; and Moroccan-spiced lamb spare ribs with apricot glaze—hints of black truffle fungi always in the background.

Inexpensive

BLT Burger
$ American Diner
Mirage, 3400 Las Vegas Blvd. S. 702-792-7888. www.bltburger.com.
You don't have to be pregnant to love the fried pickles here. Chef Laurent Tourondel delivers sinful food to Sin City. You cannot get further from your "good and should" list than milk shakes 14 ways with, or without, added kick; fries six ways including jalapeño peppers and flat waffle bites; and seven styles of burgers with or without the bun. The I'll-diet-tomorrow dessert choices include S'mores and "Krispy Kreme" doughnut bread pudding.

🌿 Canyon Ranch Café
$ Contemporary American
The Venetian, 3355 Las Vegas Blvd. S. Breakfast and Lunch. 702-414-3633. www.venetian.com.
Who says you can't eat lean in Las Vegas? At Canyon Ranch Café you'll find truly fat-defying nourishment. A member of the famed Tucson spa family, the signature café

was created by some of the most talented spa chefs and nutritionists in the nation. Enjoy pancakes with ginger-maple syrup, vegetarian stir-fry and a horseradish salmon sandwich with cranberry ketchup; all without guilt. In case you're counting, the menu lists the calorie, protein and carb counts for all dishes. The café is located off the open lobby of the 🌿 **Canyon Ranch SpaClub** *(see Spas).*

Chin Chin
$ Chinese
New York-New York, 3790 Las Vegas Blvd. S. 702-740-6300. www.newyorknewyorkcasino.com.
True to its name, which means "to your health," this California chain offers "lite" dishes—prepared with little or no oil—and uses no MSG in its food. You can watch chefs in the open exhibition kitchen whip up tasty dim sum appetizers like shredded chicken salad with red ginger dressing, and Anthony's special noodles (lo mein with chicken in a spicy cilantro sauce).

Due Forni
$-$$ Italian
Summerlin, 3555 S. Town Center Dr. 702-586-6500. Lunch and Dinner. www.DueForni.com.
It takes two ovens and two types of pizza to bring out the best in Due Forni Pizza & Wine, a must-go for an authentic slice of southern Mediterranean pie in Las Vegas. The restaurant combines imported ingredients from Italy, such as buffalo milk mozzarella and San Marzano tomatoes from the hills surrounding Mount Vesuvius, to offer an abundant selection of hot and cold appetizers, charcuterie, cheeses and inventive desserts as

well. Casual dining includes a large patio and such choices as Tartufo – a pizza that uses black truffle, parmesan crema fontina, roasted cremini and an easy baked egg. You'll be hard-pressed to find much over $14. Ask for the Sweet Buffalo Ricotta dessert for a perfect ending under 300 calories.

Pho
$ **Vietnamese**
Treasure Island. 3300 Las Vegas Blvd. S. 702-894-7111.
Tucked inside The Coffee Shop at Treasure Island, Pho is an unexpected delight and marks the only Vietnamese restaurant on The Strip. It only offers 30 seats and is a great place to catch an inexpensive meal that can be had in a hurry. Find signature Vietnamese favorites, most contained within the Pho, a base of a rich broth with vermicelli noodles, soy and fish, spices and fresh herbs. The main rice and meat dishes flow to the curries, although there is a savory selection for vegans as well. Don't miss the Vietnamese-style egg rolls that use fresh lemon grass and mint wrapped in a rubbery rice dough, and dipped in sweet and tangy chilli sauce. Most meals run at around $7.

'wichcraft
$ **American**
MGM Grand, 3799 Las Vegas, Blvd. S. 702-891-1111 or 702-891-3166. Breakfast and Lunch. www.mgmgrand.com.
Award-winning chef Tom Colicchio has brought an offshoot of his New York City sandwich shop to town, serving breakfast and lunch from 10am–6pm.
Don't miss Colicchio's signature house-roasted pork loin sandwich

wichcraft
MGM Resorts International

served warm with red cabbage and jalapeños on ciabatta bread, or his Sicilian tuna with fennel, black olives and lemon confit stuffed in a crusty baguette. Breakfast sandwiches, available all day, include skirt steak with fried eggs and oyster mushrooms on a ciabatta roll, and prosciutto with sweet butter on a baguette.

Chinatown District
$ **Asian**
Las Vegas Chinatown Plaza. 4255 Spring Mountain Rd. 702-221-8448. www.lvchinatown.com
Las Vegas has a massive Chinatown District that starts at the Plaza on Spring Mountain and Valley View west of the Strip and extends to well beyond the cross streets of Decatur and Jones. Chinese, Philippine, Korean, Thai, Taiwanese, noodle rooms and sushi bars, and Vietnamese pho kitchens all compete with eclectic and inexpensive offerings that are as varied as the languages spoken and savory seasonings applied. The district is anchored by a Monterey Park-style central square with more than a dozen outlets from tea rooms to dim sum dens to Hong Kong gourmet cafes, bringing true ethnic pride to the desert.

RESTAURANTS

BUFFETS

The search for the ultimate buffet is sport in Las Vegas, where rather than stars, buffets should be rated in the number of plates stacked at a setting. The free "chuckwagon" days of old may be over and the price of admission to these divine dining chambers is not always cheap, but it is always a bargain. A few quick tips for avoiding the buffet lines: go at off times if you can: dine before 6:30pm or after 8pm for instance. Join a player's club, play a few rounds of slots and get a free buffet voucher. It usually includes a line pass or a place in the "VIP" queue. Choose a top price buffet. The food is well worth the tariff, the service is on the money, the room is spacious and quiet, and lines are short.

The Buffet at Aria has a station serving kabobs, savories and naan. Desserts are all Jean-Philippe Maury. (*Aria, 702-590-7757; www.arialasvegas.com.*)

Bellagio serves venison, duck breast, steamed clams and king crab legs in addition to the usual buffet fare *(702-693-7111; www.bellagiolasvegas.com; $).*

Carnival World Buffet at the Rio features a moderately priced Mongolian grill where you can pick your own ingredients and have them cooked with chicken, beef or shrimp *(702-252-7777; www.playrio.com; $).*

Cravings at The Mirage has food stations where dishes are cooked to order. The dim sum station is particularly popular. Cravings is in the mid-priced tier *(702-791-1111; www.mirage.com; $-$$).*

The Buffet at TI takes the less-is-more approach and offers better quality food but less choice than might be available elsewhere.

Five food stations, Asian, Italian, barbecue, salads and desserts, offer selections such as dim sum, sushi, Korean hot pots, osso buco, barbecued ribs, and rotisserie chicken cordon blue. The price is mid-tier for an excellent presentation *(702-894-7111; www.treasureisland.com; $-$$.)*

The Flamingo's Paradise Garden Buffet has a view of the Wildlife Habitat and a prime rib, shrimp and crab buffet every night. The buffet ranks high among the lower-priced Strip buffet choices *(702-733-3111; www.flamingolasvegas.com; $).*

Le Village Buffet at Paris Las Vegas offers food stations from various French provinces, as well as an incredible assortment of pastries, and crêpes cooked to order *(702-946-7000; www.parislv.com; $$).*

M Resort Studio B Buffet has all the sparks of the best Strip buffets plus a dessert station run by Chef Jean-Claude Canestrier. Regular

The Un-Buffet

Held each Sunday at **Bally's Steakhouse**, *Bally's Sterling Brunch (702-967-7999; www.ballyslv.com; $$$)* is not a buffet in the traditional sense. The menu changes weekly, but you can always expect sturgeon caviar, Cordon Rouge champagne, fresh sushi, made-to-order omelets, oysters, beef tenderloin, lobster and hovering white-gloved waiters to cater to your concerns. A true Vegas hold-out from the glorious gourmet room days.

cooking classes held in Studio B are delicious, nutritious, informative and include buffet lunch *(M Resort, 702.797.1000; www.themresort.com. $-$$)*.

The Spice Market Buffet is possibly one of the best buffets on The Strip, revered by locals and visitors alike. Find aromatic specialties here such as tandoori chicken and Middle Eastern salads, fresh hot and cold crabs legs, a wok station that does not overcook and over saturate the contents, a Mongolian barbecue, even cherries jubilee inside a copious dessert bar *(702-785-5555; www.planet hollywood.com; $$)*.

The Feast Buffets at Station Casino Resorts are a local's secret in Las Vegas. The prices are right, the selections run from common to haute, the desserts are plentiful and creative and there are always a mix of ethnic tasting stations, from Mongolian grill to Mexican to prime rib. Don't expect unlimited crabs legs, though—another casualty of the recession.

Find Feast Buffets at **Green Valley Ranch** *(702-617-7777)*, **Sunset Station** *(702-547-7777)*, **Boulder Station** *(702-432-7777)*, **Palace Station** *(702-367-2411)*, **Santa Fe Station** *(702-658-4900)*, **Texas Station** *(702-631-1000)*, and **Red Rock Casino Resort** *(702-797-7777; www.stationcasinos.com;$)*.

Red Rock's Feast is especially popular for its **Sunday Champagne Brunch** from 8am–4pm.

House of Blues Sunday Gospel Brunch is not quite the most expensive buffet in town but certainly the most entertaining. It's a must for the cornbread and coffee crowd who want some spirit with those eggs. Both the 10am and 1pm seatings bring bottomless mimosas to wash down hickory — smoked bacon, cheese-laced grits, and bourbon-soaked ham, and all the belting sound you can handle. *(Mandalay Bay; 702-632-7600; www.hob.com/venues/clubvenues/ lasvegas/gospelbrunch.asp; $$)*.

The Village Seafood Buffet at Rio is the city's only true seafood buffet. If you want seafood some two hundred ways, this is the right place. Chef Richard Leggett who hails from the Ritz-Carlton in Buckhead, GA, is quick to point out 84 hot food dishes on the line, as well as 96 cold dishes (including salads and sushis) and 51 desserts. The buffet reopened in March 2008 after a $12 million, total design revamp to make the décor match the $38 per person admission *(open daily for dinner only)*.

Harrah's Buffet of Buffets has a deal that provides unlimited, any-time admission to any or all of the buffets within the Harrah's family for $44.95 (+ tax) per 24-hour period. For those who want to dine around, eat a lot and keep their wallets from getting too thin, the full-day buffet pass gives you access to nine buffets: **Lago Buffet** (Caesars); **Le Village Buffet** (Paris); **Spice Market Buffet** (Planet Hollywood); **Flavors Buffet** (Harrah's); **Paradise Garden Buffet** (Flamingo); **Carnival World Buffet** (The Rio); **Village Seafood Buffet** (The Rio, add $15 per visit at this venue) and **Emperor's Buffet** (Imperial Place).

Caveat: You may spend many of those 24 hours on line as the buffet pass does not include a VIP line pass *(www.caesars.com/buffets)*.

RESTAURANTS BY THEME

Looking for the best meal deal in town? Want to dine where the glitterati go? Need the right place for that special occasion? Las Vegas is fast becoming a culinary capital of the world's top chefs, and that means abundant competition for your dining dollar. In the preceding pages, we've organized restaurants by price category, so here we've broken them out by theme to help you plan just the right evening out.

CUT

Jeff Green/The Palazzo

MUST EAT

Alizé

Andre's Las Vegas

RESTAURANTS

145

HOTELS

The properties listed below were selected for their ambience, location and value for money. Prices reflect the average cost for a standard double room for two people (not including applicable taxes, including the city's 8.10% hotel tax). Hotels in Las Vegas constantly offer special discount rates. Properties are located in Las Vegas, unless otherwise specified. For a listing of additional casino hotels, see Casinos. See the end of this section for a list of hotels by theme. **The Michelin Guide** has more recommended hotels.

Luxury **$$$$$** over $350   *Moderate* **$$$** $175-$250

Expensive **$$$$** $250-$350   *Inexpensive* **$ –$$** $100-$175

Strip view room, Mandarin Oriental

Mandarin Oriental Hotel Group

Luxury

Bellagio

$$$$$ **3,933 rooms**

3600 Las Vegas Blvd. S.

702-693-7444 or 888-987-6667.

www.bellagio.com

Originally Steve Wynn's prized property when it opened in 1998 it had all the magnificence Las Vegas could offer: a mesmerizing fountain show display, rose-trellised pool gardens, marble corridors filled with the sound of Italian romance arias, a French greenhouse conservatory dedicated to grand botanical artistry, casino lounges featuring a concert pianist and caviar on the menu…. It just didn't get better than this for Las Vegas and is still a hard bet to beat.

Four Seasons Hotel Las Vegas

$$$$$ **424 rooms**

3960 Las Vegas Blvd. S.

702-632-5000 or 877-632-5000.

www.fourseasons.com.

One of the only hotels on The Strip without a casino, Four Seasons maintains its distinctive identity even though its rooms occupy the 36th to 39th floors of adjoining Mandalay Bay. Spacious rooms are done in wood and rattan with floor-to-ceiling windows looking out on the mountains and desert.

For a memorable dining experience, try the artisan-aged beef at **Charlie Palmer Steak ($$$)**.

Mandarin Oriental

$$$$$ **392 rooms**
3752 Las Vegas Blvd. S.
702-590-8888 or 888-881-9578.
www.mandarinoriental.com/
lasvegas.

This is one of the few places in the US where you can stay at a Mandarin Oriental with the full luxury experience offered by the Hong Kong-based company without breaking the bank. As with other luxury elements of Las Vegas, the company has learned the discount or die philosophy of the gaming mecca and often puts together deals and creative packaging that will make the experience possible for those who would not normally consider this option. The rooms offer stunning Asian accents; service is superb; the lobby, 23rd floor, serves tea at 4pm with views over The Strip.

🏊 Skylofts at MGM Grand

$$$$$ **51 loft suites**
3799 Las Vegas Blvd. S.
877-646 638.
www.skylotsmgmgrand.com.

The 51 super-luxe lofts in the MGM Grand penthouse are actually a hotel within a hotel with their own elevator entrance, check-in desk and concierge. Anyone with a grand or (a lot) more to spend on a night in neon heaven above The Strip can have it all in a town that does it all, no holds barred. The 1,400- to 6,000-square-foot 1, 2 and 3-bedroom, split-level lofts come with an army of built-ins, such as floor-to-ceiling two-story windows, custom Bang & Olufsen and loaded Sony HDTV audio-visual equipment, espresso machines with custom selection of exclusive coffees (and fine herbal teas);

custom-designed radio-controlled remote panels to operate TV, DVD, radio, CD, internet radio, drapes, temperature and lights; high-speed internet access and Anichini and Fili D'Oro linens. This is Vegas à la Georges V or Cipriani, over neon rather than Belle Epoche or Renaissance walkways. Have your Champagne at the bar.

Expensive

🏊 Cosmopolitan★

$$$$ **2,995 rooms**
3708 Las Vegas Blvd. S.
702-215-5500 or 877-551-7778.
www.cosmopolitanlasvegas.com.

Call it feisty, call it sexy, call it artsy. Cosmopolitan, the newest tower on the canyon called the Las Vegas Strip has earned its urban sizzle by producing a resort that dazzles and confounds no matter where you place your eyes. The lobby is a labyrinth of continuously morphing video art, shadowed by a gossamer web or is it an all-consuming layer cake of crystal dripping from the ceiling heights. Take elevators to the mezzanine to find odd art displays, such as a behemoth red stiletto heal shoe or 1950s cigarette machines dispensing hand-sized artworks for $5 a pull. Rooms, too, keep the wows coming. These are

Lobby, Cosmopolitan of Las Vegas

HOTELS

50 floors of what was intended to be residences so they are large layouts of glass overlooking the neon with terraces over the action. The property is getting known as a new scene spot with pool parties and concerts that draw the crowds. Dining, too, is a deal here with some top name finds: David Meyers' Comme Ca, Scott Conant's Scarpetta and D.O.C.G., Jose Andres' China Poblana, and The One Group's STK Steakhouse..

Wynn Las Vegas
$$$ **3,933 rooms**
3131 Las Vegas Blvd. S.
702-770-7000 or 877-321-WYNN.
www.wynnlasvegas.com.
This eponymous ode to the man who made Vegas is a gem on The Strip across (and connected by a bridge) to the Fashion Show Mall. Enter and you will see traces of Bellagio. Wynn employed many of the same designers. The Chihuly glass flower garden illuminated by a skylight is one of the initial bursts of beauty to encounter. And then there is the Lake of Dreams with its mountain of pines and waterfalls that engage a stunning sound and light performance come sundown. Rooms here are stunning too, design intensive with all sorts of artistic touches and ornaments (as well as bedding) that can be purchased in the hotel's own home store. Always a lover of art, pieces of Wynn's personal collection—Picasso, Renoir, Matisse and Monet—hang in retrospective behind the registration desk if you care to lift your eyes. The resort also features a championship Pete Dye-designed golf course with a splendid 17th hole. It's the only course on The Strip.

Wynn Encore Las Vegas
$$$$ **2,034 rooms**
3121 Las Vegas Blvd. S.
702-770-8000 or 888-320-7125
www.encorelasvegas.com.
Encore connects to Wynn Las Vegas in an almost seamless line of Chinese reds, burnt oranges, blues and whites that will wake up your senses and have you following the butterflies that act as the going motif for this spot. The rooms here are snazzier and bigger than Wynn's—suites actually that measure in at 700 square feet for the standard option. Plenty of glass, original art (check out the Botero's at the same-name restaurant) and creative spaces here—such as can be found at the restaurant Switch where the ambient walls switch scenes and decorative properties every 20 minutes. There is also a dining venue dedicated to Sinatra with his sounds, his photos, his awards and a continuous films displaying. The Encore Spa reflects many of the Oriental tones that Wynn spa embraces, but, as is the case with much about this hotel, it just does it better, goes farther and takes the task to the next tier.

Moderate

Aria at CityCenter
$$$$ **4,004 rooms**
3730 Las Vegas Blvd. S.
702-590-7111 or 866-359-7757.
www.arialasvegas.com.
Aria is the anchor of the 67-acre complex called CityCenter and it is a sweeping testimony to the future focused technology and forward-thinking design elements that allowed Dubai World to come in as a partner and make it all it could be. It displays all of its LEED

awards proudly on the mezzanine landing, but you will sense the green attitude immediately when you step into the crowded casino and do not smash into a wall of cigarette smoke. A complex, yet simple filtering system built into all the slot banks captures smoke and buries it before it ever reaches the air supply. Another element that predominates is art. You'll see it in commissioned works all over CityCenter and especially in the work called Silver River, an 80-foot long sculpture in Silver by Maya Lin on the wall of the lobby. Head past the striking display of colorful stacked boxes and giant cupcakes that decorate Jean-Philippe Maury's chocolate bar and up the escalator to Elvis, a wild and wonderful ode to The King by Cirque du Soleil and find the city's only dedicated Elvis shop, full of souvenirs, from Elvis watches and cups to lunch boxes and Pez heads. Rooms are decked with modern touch design elements and a bedside console that, if you figure it out, ensures you need only lift a finger to work the room.

M Resort

$$$ **390 rooms**
12300 Las Vegas Blvd. S.
702-796-1000 or 877-673-7678
www.themresort.com.
A glass ship-like building somewhat out in the middle of nowhere, M Resort is actually the perfect place to be. Located far south of the action on The Strip, M Resort is its own little orbit, near enough to The Strip and the entertaining shopping to be found at Town Square and far enough away from the madding crowd. Every room, modern and

spacious, has a floor to ceiling view of the desert expanse. The casino and public areas are rarely over-crowded. The space is clean-edged, voluminous and chock full of worthy venues to explore: Hostile Grape with its wine dispensers offering DIY wine tastings starting at $2 a glass. There's Hash House a Go-Go where breakfasts of chicken fried steak and French toast are as sinful and extravagant as they sound. Take cooking and nutrition classes at Studio B, including a buffet lunch. Afterwards, a pool spread provides the opium beds and day life without the beer, breasts and booze crowd.

Palazzo

$$$ **3,066 rooms**
3355 Las Vegas Blvd. S.
877-883-6423 or 7 02-414-1000.
www.palazzolasvegas.com.
This sprawling manor of a resort connects to The Venetian and the Venezia tower to turn the total complex into the largest hotel complex in the world with a total of 7,093 rooms. The Palazzo opened in 2009 as the crowning piece of the Venetian complex. The casino, unlike most similar venues in Vegas, is large and spacious with wide straight corridors to navigate and an ambience you might rather find off a piazza in Monte Carlo. Rooms are comfortable, luxurious places to take respite with designer brand bath amenities, contemporary Euro-style furnishings, lavish linens and bedding and a step-down living room with a corner for office amenities. An army of top chef talent mans the dining venues: Mario Batali, Wolfgang Puck, Charlie Trotter… and a three-floor luxury shopping mall with stores

149

such as Barney's, Tory Burch, Christian Louboutin, and Diane Von Furstenberg, connects Palazzo to The Venetian and the rambling and atmospheric Canal Shoppes there. Canyon Ranch Spa club runs a 134,000 square foot spa that connects The Venetian and Palazzo and leads out to a meandering pool area.

Signature at MGM Grand
$$$ **1,695 suites**
145 East Harmon Ave.
702-797-6000 or 877-612-2121.
www.signaturemgmgrand.com.
The Signature is MGM Grand's answer to solid ground. Three 38-story towers, a partnership between MGM Mirage and the Turnberry Group, connect to MGM by moving walkway, putting all the nightlife, restaurants, entertainment and action of the Resort and The Strip within shouting distance. But the Signature is a bit of a retreat from all that. The suites here are comfortable and efficient, featuring top of the line kitchen appliances, large granite bathrooms, often a fireplace and balcony and wide views of the valley. Each property has its own pool if the 6.5-acre Grand pool complex seems like too much. You can also find Starbuck's and other amenities in the lobby. Suites are non-smoking and a good value in Las Vegas for convenience and cost, especially for families.

Tropicana
$$$ **1,874 rooms**
3801 Las Vegas Blvd. S.
702-739-2222 or 888-826-8767.
www.troplv.com.
The tropical-themed property that rose from the dust in 1960 to become one of the kingpins of Las Vegas Boulevard—only to take a dive in the 1990s as a wasteland with low ceilings, florescent lights and a sort of slimy slot-house charm—has risen again to a certain splendor. In fact, the dust is still settling on the Trop's new South Beach bright $165-million redo. Rooms are smart and sassy with sharp colors and plantation-style appointments. Gone are the parrots and the snaking lagoon pool. In are Nikki Beach and an impressive new mob museum attraction. If you're looking for the buffet, that's gone too. You'll have to make do with a fancy white clothed joint called Biscayne that offers four-course, wine paired meals for $39.99. Shades of the old dame still appear now and then – the Tiffany firmament above the casino for one. And the tiki weding hut is another. You can check it out when you head to Nikki Café for brunch.

 Trump Las Vegas
$$-$$$ **1,282 suites**
200 Fashion Show Dr.
702-982-0000 or 866-646-8164.
www.trumplasvegashotel.com.
The Trump touch is apparent the minute you step into this

Trump Las Vegas

Trump Las Vegas

new 64-story high-rise along The Strip: an expansive, marble lobby illuminated by crystal chandeliers, no lines at the check-in counter, no intrusions from the sounds of slots—in fact there is no casino at all here. Trump offers a bit of dignity on The Strip and complements it with non-smoking suites that pack all the comforts of home—even if it is someone else's home. This is a condo-hotel and keeping the owners (and guests) happy is the name of the game. To do that, Trump offers 24-hour room service and concierge service, a full service luxury 🛁 **spa**, a calming high tea session in the afternoon and splendid cocktails just before dinner. It's a bit of upper West Side on The Strip, steps away from "Fifth Avenue" shopping at 🛁 **Fashion Show Mall**.

Vdara at CityCenter
$$$ 1,495 rooms
2600 W. Harmon Ave.
702-590-2111 or 866-745-7767.
www.vdara.com.

The curvy come hither of Vdara sets up a promised sexiness that is met inside with bold art pieces, a classy bar and patio lounge, a bold and exotic restaurant and the absence of two things difficult to avoid in Vegas: smoking and gambling. From the start you know Vdara is smart. But the wow here goes beyond, bold color schemes and over-the-top designs. Vdara is much more subtle than that. Rather, it's the rooms that count here. They are all suites, they all have cleverly designed kitchens and efficient and precious dining spaces, and they are all designed to be LEED forward models of what shelters

should be. Smart design is also comely here with custom-designed king beds, plush linens, dual nightlights, expansive windows and clean-lined furnishings. Spa Vdara offers a champagne bar and a menu of environmentally friendly treatments. And there is a pool, of course, on a lower rooftop overlooking the urban flow of CityCenter. Keep an eye out for the art. Frank Stella behind the registration desk; Peter Wegner's "Day for Night, Night for Day" by the elevators.

🛁 The Venetian
$$$ 4,027 rooms
3355 Las Vegas Blvd. S.
702-414-1000 or 877-883-6423.
www.venetian.com.

The Venetian followed in a line of luxury leaders when it opened at the end of the last decade. The property was an ode to a romance the owner shared with his new bride when they honeymooned in Venice and decided they had to take some of that home with them. The property is a symphony in Murano glass, Italian marble floors, finely crafted faux frescos and skillful design that dutifully resurrects some of the sites to behold in the City of Canals. Find a Bridge of Sighs, a clock tower, the Doge's Palace, even a mini St. Mark's Square. It's all tastefully done in a larger enough sprawl for one to pause and marvel from point to point without getting walked into. The casino is crowded, but that can make the game more exciting. Standard rooms average 700 square feet in stuffy and heavy Italian style décor, each quarters possessing a step-down living room and large marble bathroom.

A stay at the Venetian means plenty of choice—from some two dozen dining venues, the largest hotel spa on The Strip, if not the world, pools aplenty, nightlife and an on-site Broadway musical: Phantom of the Opera in a custom created opera house of its own.

Inexpensive

Artisan Hotel
$ –$$ **64 rooms**
1501 W Sahara Ave.
702-214-4000 or 800-554-4092.
www.theartisanhotel.com.
This handsomely decorated boutique hotel is an unusual find for visitors who want to try something other than a megaresort on The Strip. A Mediterranean style provides a smattering of peace with comfortable opium style chaises and shady cabanas. There's a lounge on-site with DJ action on weekends. Champagne brunch on weekends makes for a fancy affair without the fancy prices.
The location is good near both The Strip and shopping.

Rumor
$$ **390 rooms**
455 East Harmon Ave. 702-369-5400. www.rumorvegas.com.
What's old in Vegas is new again if you stick around long enough. In this case, the former St. Tropez motel is now has a new life as Rumor, a purplish property that is not afraid to make some buzz. Find 10-foot glass elevators, low lying, leather geometric banquettes accented by a 1960s Champagne effect here, and maybe a 007 psychedelic chic effect there. It's all about compact space and having fun with it. The on-site restaurant,

Addiction serves breakfast, lunch, dinner. The grounds include a rolling grass lawn with hammocks, a pool with weekend DJ and even a dog park. Guestrooms keep the quirkiness going with purple accents, gothic mirrors and chandeliers—and the whole house can be rented for the night for a mere $15,000, including DJ.

⚓ Golden Nugget
$ –$$ **1,907 rooms**
129 East Fremont St.
702-385-7111or 800-846-5336.
www.goldennugget.com.
Downtown's largest hotel was acquired by Landry's Restaurant Corp. in 2005 and given a $100-million redo that put sharks in the middle of the pool, new restaurants and lounges around the hotel, new softgoods in the rooms, new suites to reserve and a new VIP check-in area for those who want to pay a premium for more personalized service. The even newer Rush Tower comes with huge designer rooms, new restaurant venues and plenty of panache. The property has the only full-service spa in Downtown and features two Starbuck's onsite. A nightclub overlooks the neon promenade on Fremont St.

Standard Room, Rush Tower, Golden Nugget

Golden Nugget Hotel & Casino

HOTELS BY THEME

Looking for a hip hangout in Las Vegas or a quiet place off The Strip? Want a good bargain, or need a business hotel? In the preceding pages, we've organized the properties by price category, so below we've broken them out by theme to help you plan your trip.

Standard Suite, Vdara at CityCenter

CityCenter/MGM Resorts International

Best Bang for the Buck
Artisan *p 152*
Golden Nugget *p 152*
Rumor *p 152*
Signature *p 150*
Trump Las Vegas *p 150*
Vdara . *p51, p 151*

For Business Travelers
Four Seasons *p 146*
Trump Las Vegas *p 150*
Vdara *p 151*

Hotels with Hip Décor
Artisan *p 152*
Rumor *p 152*
Skylofts *p 147*

Off The Strip
Artisan *p 152*
Four Seasons Hotel *p 146*
Golden Nugget *p 152*
Rumor *p 152*
M Resort *p 149*
Signature *p 150*

No Casino
Artisan *p 152*
Four Seasons Hotel *p 146*
Rumor *p 152*
Signature *p 150*
Trump Las Vegas *p 150*
Mandarin Oriental *p 147*
Vdara *p 151*

Spa Experiences
Aria *p 148*
Bellagio *p 146*
Four Seasons Las Vegas *p 146*
Wynn Encore *p 148*
Mandarin Oriental *p 147*
Golden Nugget *p 152*
Trump Las Vegas *p 150*
Vdara *p 151*
Venetian *p 151*
Wynn *p 148*

Vegas Classics
Golden Nugget *p 152*
Tropicana *p 150*

Way Off The Strip
M Resort *p 149*

HOTELS

153

LAS VEGAS

The following abbreviations may appear in this Index:
NHS National Historic Site; **NM** National Monument; **NMem** National Memorial; **NP** National Park; **NHP** National Historical Park; **NRA** National Recreational Area; **NWR** National Wildlife Refuge; **SP** State Park; **SHP** State Historical Park; **SHS** State Historic Site.

INDEX

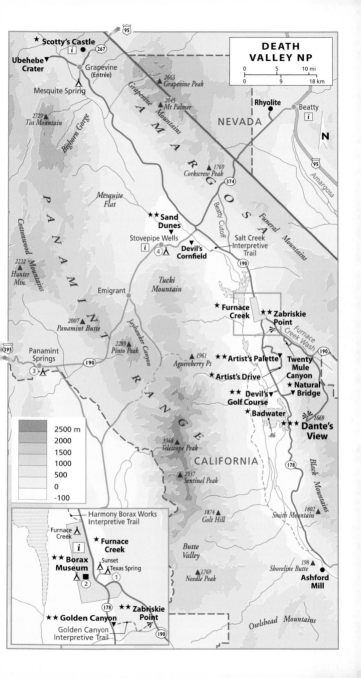